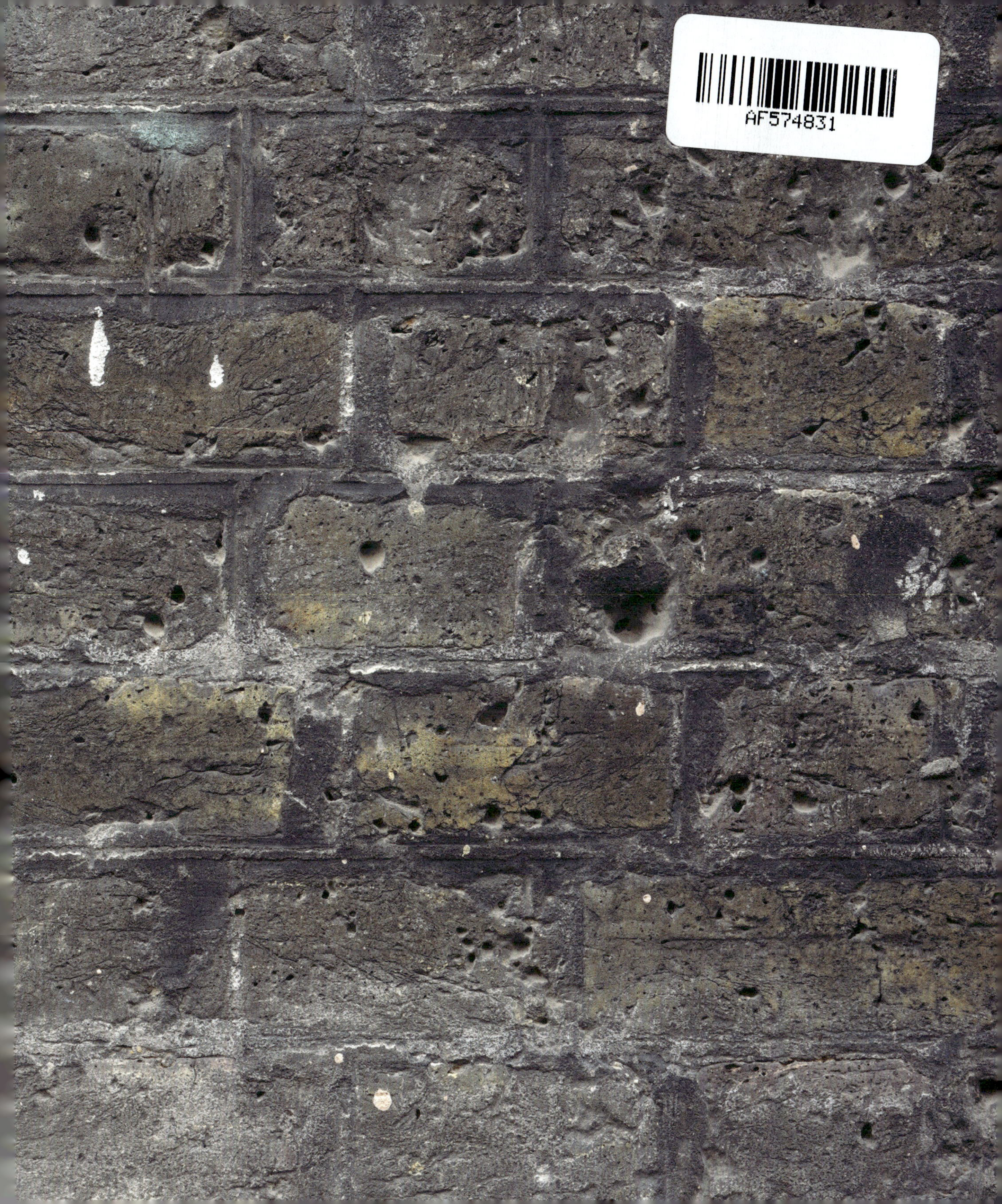

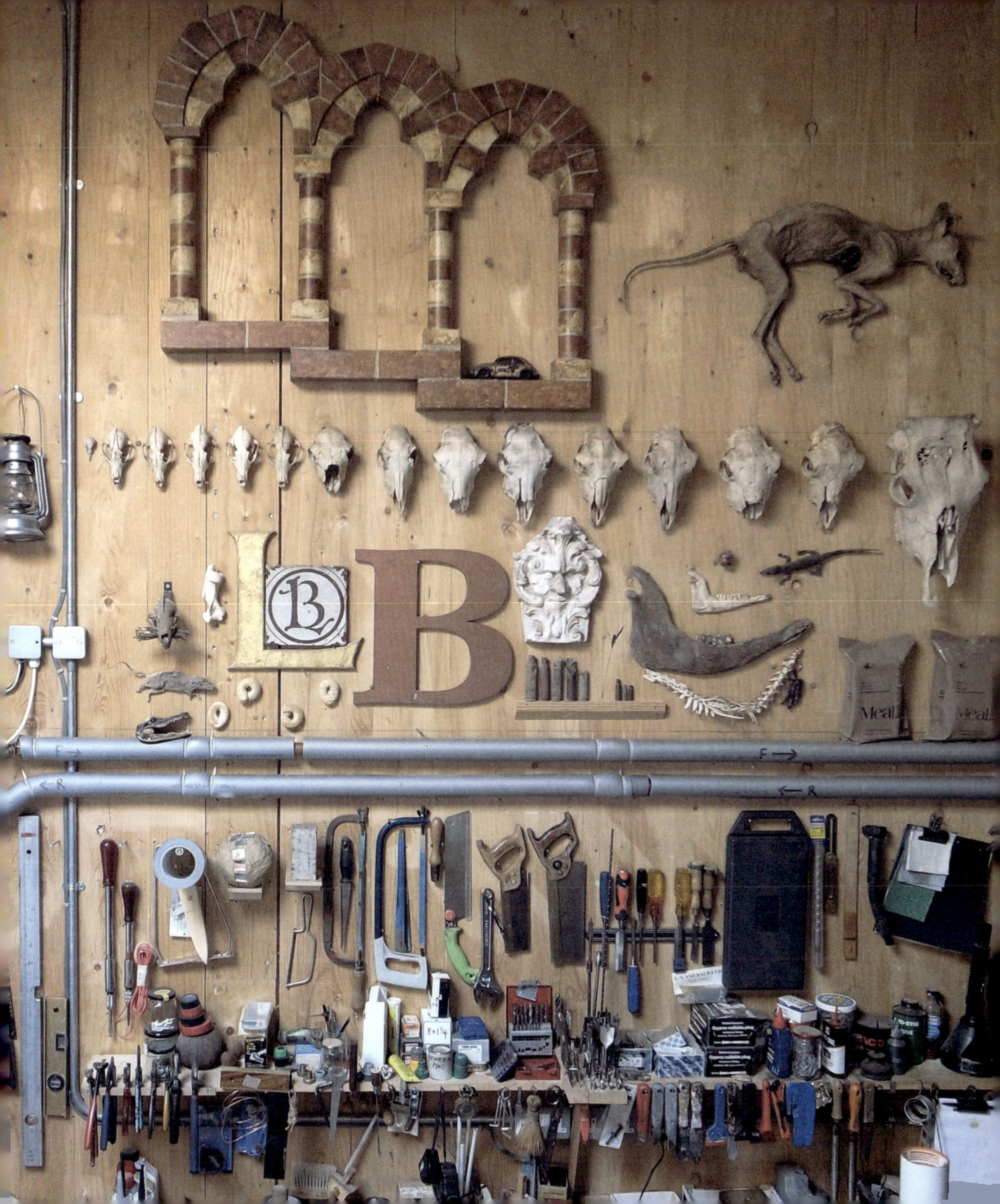

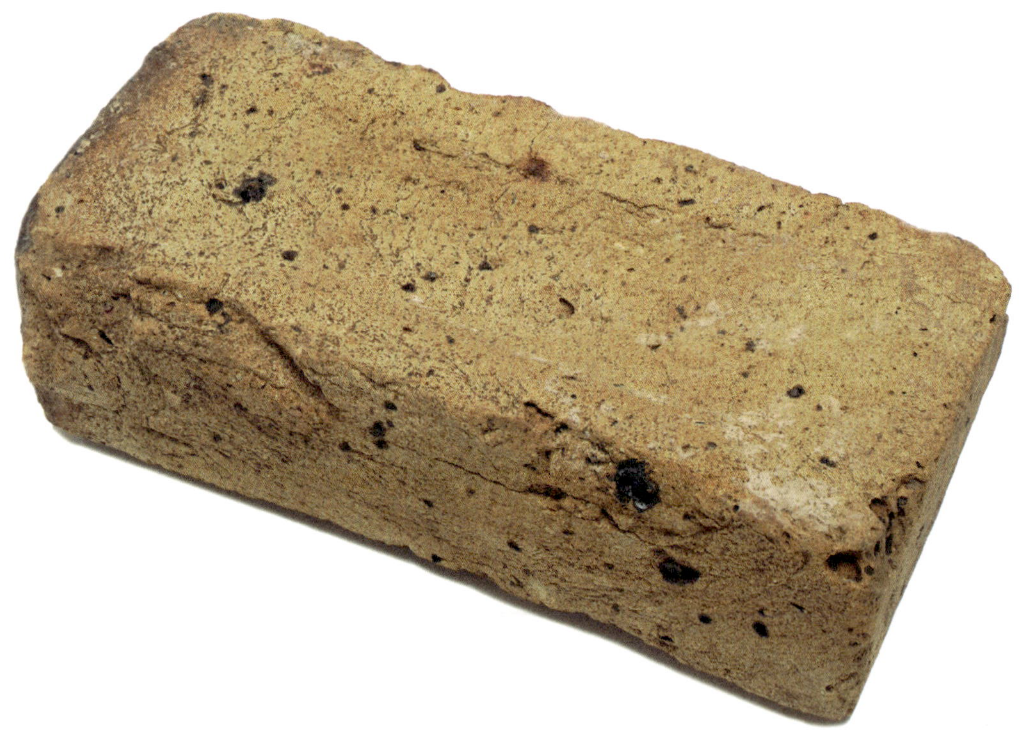

Langlands & Bell
Degrees of Truth

Sir John Soane's Museum

Langlands & Bell
Degrees of Truth
4 March – 31 May 2020

This exhibition has been made possible thanks to the support of Pomellato, Thompson & Caroline Dean, and Christian & Florence Levett.

Published by Sir John Soane's Museum
13 Lincoln's Inn Fields
London WC 2A 3BP
+44 (0)20 7405 2107
www.soane.org
Registered charity no. 313609

Editor Owen Hopkins
Editorial assistance Erin McKellar
Design Herman Lelie
Layouts Stefania Bonelli
Repro Dexter Pre-Media
Printing EBS, Italy

Photo credits: pp.1, 2, 8, 10, 11, 14, 18, 30, 42–43, 47, 49, 50, 63, 64–65, 66–67, 71, 72–73, 74–75, 77, 78 (top, bottom), 79, 82–83, 84, 86 (bottom), 88, 89, 92–93, 96: Langlands & Bell; pp.15, 40: Edward Woodman; pp.16: Photo: Steve White, digital artwork: Richard Wilding; pp.19, 20, 21: Peter White; pp.23, 24, 56, 57: Digital artwork: Richard Wilding; pp.27, 28: Steve White; pp.29: Jörg Sasse; pp.33: © Richard Waite; pp.35 (top, bottom), 37 (bottom): Langlands & Bell in association with V/Space LAB; pp.37 (top): Photo © Tate: *The Old Library Staircase*, 1827, Joseph Mallord William Turner (1775–1851). Accepted by the nation as part of the Turner Bequest 1856; pp.39, 62: Prudence Cummings Associates; pp.46, 68, 76, 86 (top): © Sir John Soane's Museum; pp.51: Photo © Tate: *Adjoining Rooms*, 1989, Langlands & Bell (b. 1955 and 1959). Tate, presented by Doris Lockhart-Saatchi through the Contemporary Art Society 2005; pp.52: photo still missing; pp.54, 55, 59, 60: Digital artwork: Richard Wilding, published by Alan Cristea Gallery, London; pp.80, 81: Gareth Winters

British Library Cataloguing in Publication Data
A catalogue record for this book is available from the British Library

ISBN 978-1-9996932-3-7

Cover: **Starfish** 2020
Front end papers: Brickwork at 40 Myrdle Street, Whitechapel, London, 2019
Back end papers: Brickwork at 12 Lincoln's Inn Fields, London, 2019
p.1: Wall of studio workshop at **Untitled**, Kent, 2010
Frontispiece: London yellow stock brick, 1986

Contents

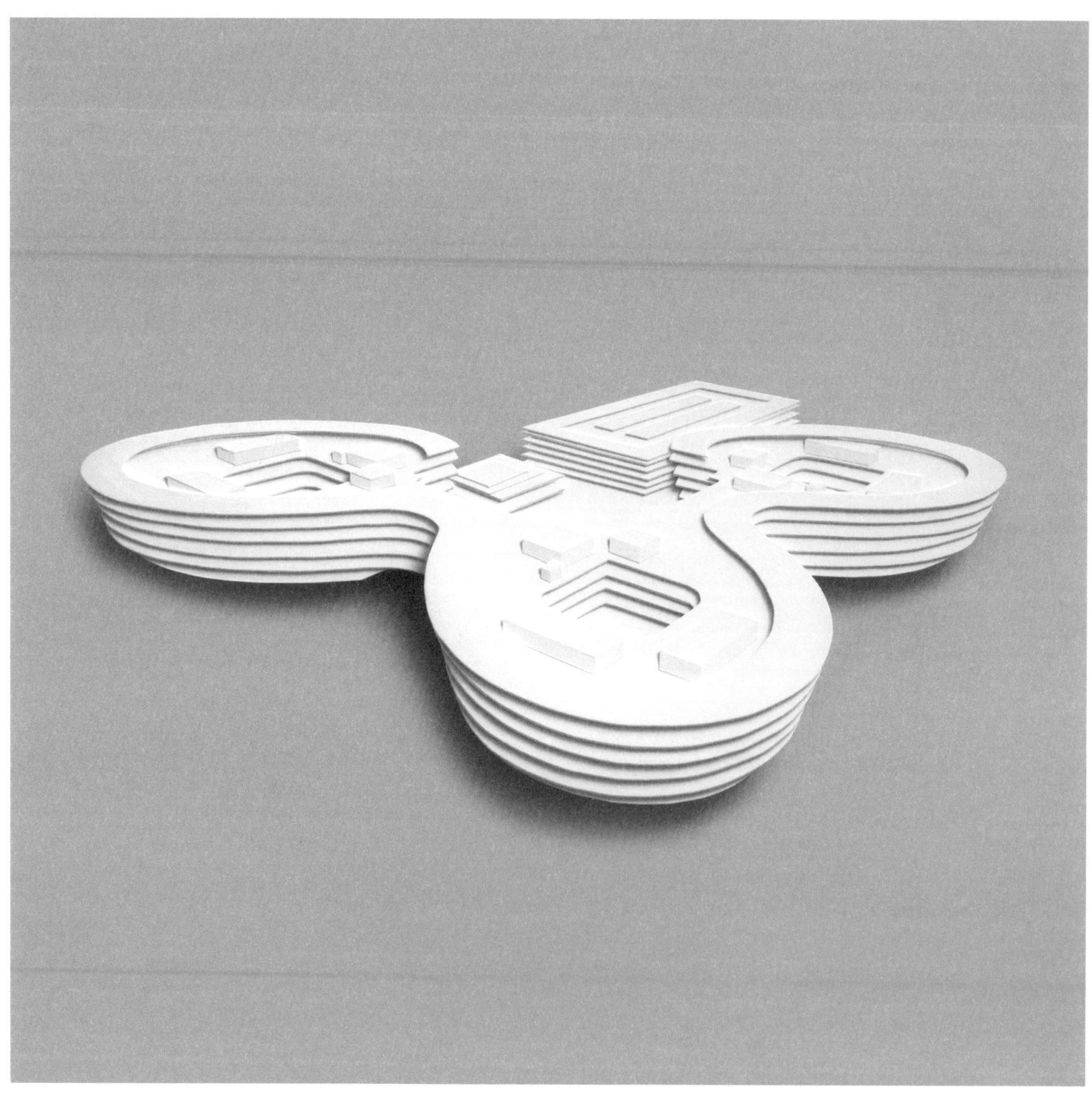

Apple, Sunny Vale 2017

Foreword

In one of his last poems, 'The Circus Animals' Desertion', William Butler Yeats identified the source of inspiration in the everyday, 'the sweepings of a street, old kettles, old bottles, and a broken can'– all transformed by the artist's imagination into 'masterful images'. It is through a similar alchemy that Langlands & Bell create their art, with a vision that extends from the structures we inhabit to the networks and systems of communication that shape the contemporary world.

Thus it is a great pleasure to welcome Ben Langlands and Nikki Bell to Sir John Soane's Museum, for their approach to art and architecture resonates with that of our founder. Indeed, their works on display resonate with the building because, like Soane, they employ objects to conjure up an overlooked world, a kind of urban archaeology that looks both forward and back, much as Soane deployed his fragments to recreate a lost landscape of antiquity while also speculating on an imagined future.

An exhibition like *Degrees of Truth* could only be realised through the generosity of its lenders: Tate, Southampton City Art Gallery, and Ipswich City Museum & Art Gallery, as well as Christina and Dimitri Goulandris, DJ Lockhart, Derwent London plc, Cristea Roberts Gallery, private collectors, and the artists themselves. We are also most grateful for the generous support of Pomellato, and to Thompson & Caroline Dean, and Christian & Florence Levett, all of whom have made this exhibition possible.

Bruce Boucher, FSA
Deborah Loeb Brice Director

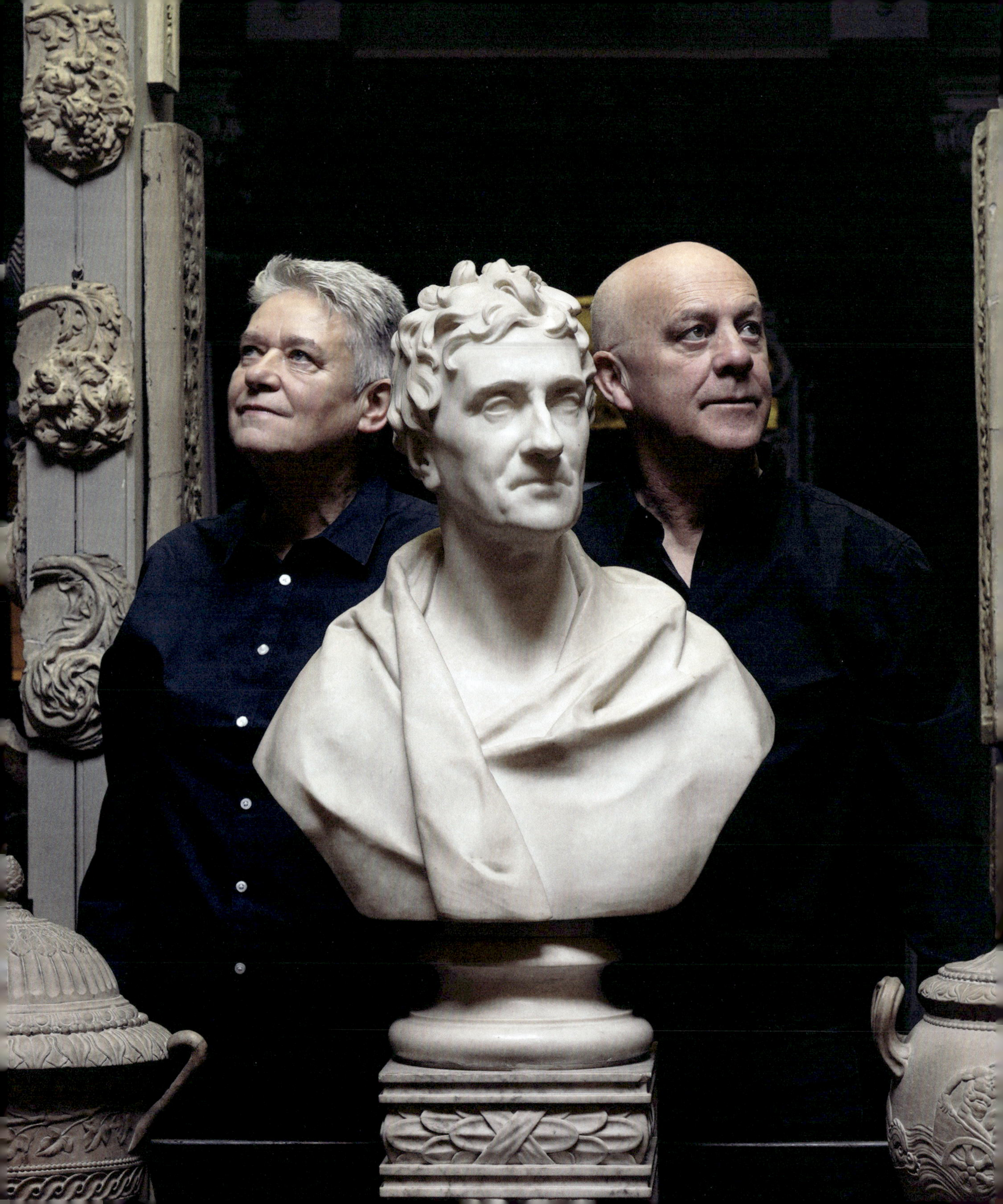

Degrees of Truth

A conversation between Langlands & Bell ○ and exhibition curator, Owen Hopkins ◇

Two houses

○ We were walking through the city one day and we suddenly came across a statue looking down at us from the perimeter wall of the Bank of England.

◇ To someone who has been to and knows Sir John Soane's Museum it's a familiar face – the one that peers out across the Dome Area at the heart of the Museum. But at the Bank of the England the depiction is curiously outside of time. The face has very obviously been copied from the bust by Sir Francis Chantrey, but then you have this rigid, austerely neo-classical body, the sweeping cloak, and the vaguely Soanean decorative motifs around. It's part of Herbert Baker's redevelopment of Soane's Bank of England in the 1920s – a weird token of apology for destroying his masterwork – one of the corollaries of which is that the Soane Museum achieves pre-eminent status as Soane's greatest achievement – architectural or otherwise.

○ We first came to the Museum in the early 1980s. We discovered it soon after we bought a ruined eighteenth-century house in Whitechapel at auction, which we then restored. It had a wood-panelled interior, but the exterior was this very typically, yellow brick, late eighteenth-century London terraced house – beautiful but very basic. It wasn't a grand house. It was a modest house in Whitechapel, built in the 1790s and was only meant to last 60 years, but it was still very serviceable. We loved its beautiful details, and the ones that were missing we tried to restore or put back. Over time, the house became an extension of ourselves, we displayed work within it that related to the East End and our relationship with it – the house itself was on display.

So, we could instantly relate to the Soane Museum when we came here, even though it was on a grander, much more educated scale. Because we were displaying our own work and our own finds in our house, and we were learning intuitively about how the buildings were built, we felt this affinity with what Soane created.

Langlands & Bell with bust of Sir John Soane by Sir Francis Chantrey, 2019

◇ It's an interesting coincidence that your house and 12 Lincoln's Inn Fields, the first part of the Soane Museum, were built in the 1790s – though, of course, the two houses would have rather different subsequent histories.

○ The front wall of our house was fractured by a bomb that had fallen next door in 1942, so the restoration work we had to do was substantial. We rebuilt the front wall above the ground floor. We didn't have enough money to order new windows to be made. They were six-over-six sliding sashes, so we took them apart, taking each pane of glass out and rebuilding the wooden frames and replacing the bits that were rotten. We did this more or less in the dark – we had a single light bulb.

One evening we were working on the house, which was open with all the windows out, and we noticed this old man standing outside in the street. He just stood there looking up, so I leant out the window and said 'hello, can I help you?' 'I always stop outside this house when I'm in the area', he replied, 'the happiest days of my life were spent in this house. I'm glad to see you looking after it.' The conversation continued: 'I was born in 1911', he said, 'my mother brought me back here when I was two weeks old, and my earliest memories are of my mother organising the street party at the end of the First World War.' 'Nice to see you looking after it', he said again and off he went.

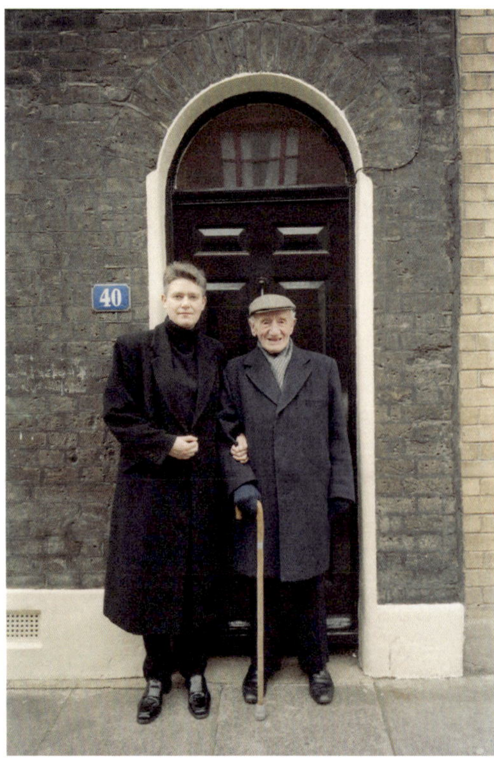

Nikki Bell with David Gold outside 40 Myrdle Street, Whitechapel, 2000

Façade of 40 Myrdle Street, Whitechapel, London, c.1992

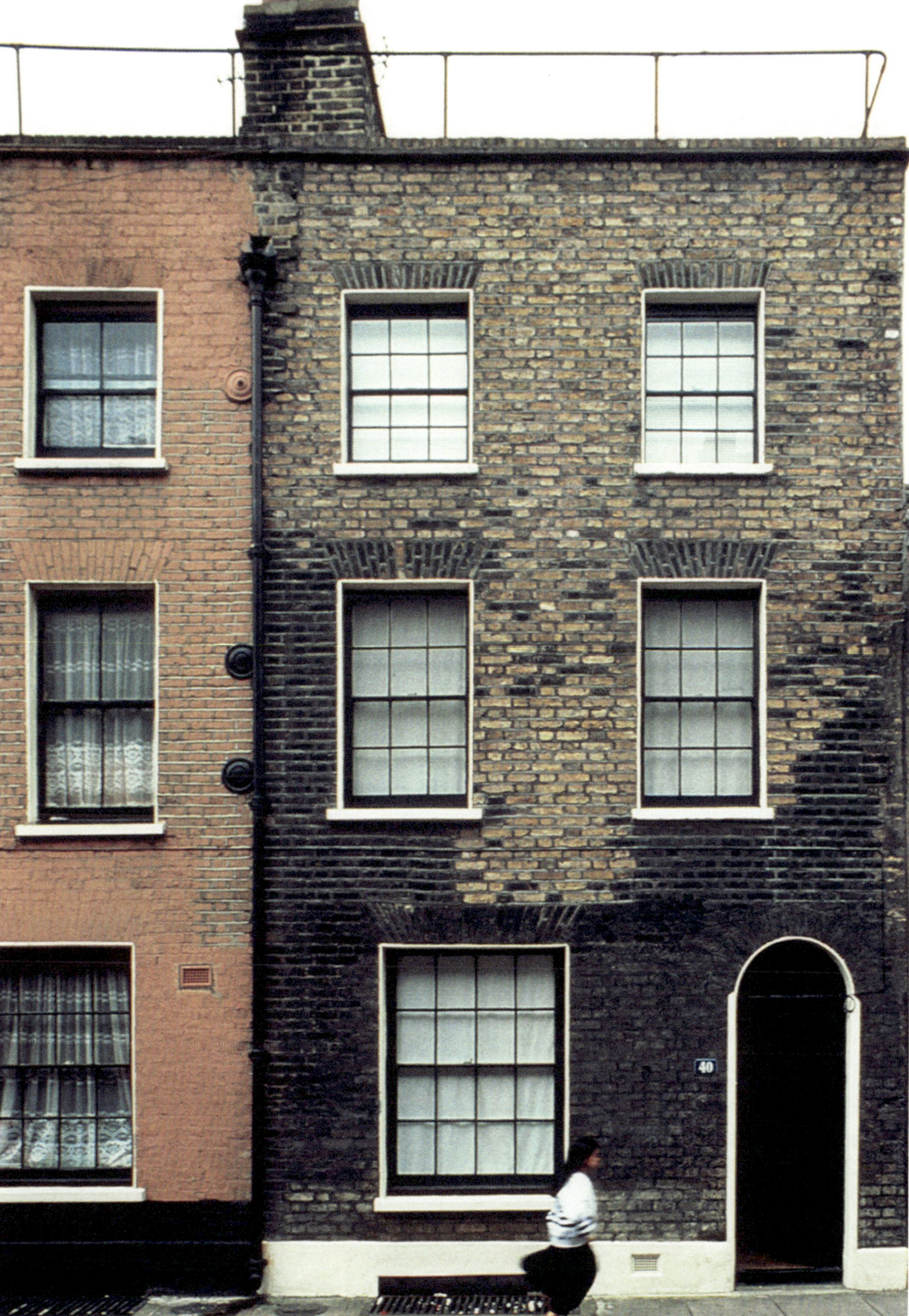
40

We never saw him again – and assumed that he lived somewhere a long way away – until years later in 2000, we were just going out of the house and there he was.

By then he was really old, but it was unmistakably him, just standing outside the house in exactly the same position, just looking at it. We said hello to each other, and he said, 'I always look at this house. When I'm in this area I always come down here. I used to live here, and we had to move out when the bomb landed next door, broke all our windows.' Remembering the conversation we had years before, we invited him inside.

We had been just about to go out, but we weren't in a rush and had time to show him the house. So we unlocked the door again, and he went in ahead of us, and it was the most amazing experience because you could feel the energy of his own memories, and all of those years – he left in 1942 – so it was six decades – rushing through and flooding back through his consciousness. We could feel it bodily, ourselves.

He walked into the ground-floor room that we used as a dining room and sitting room, and he just stood there, and he looked around. The old iron ranges were still in the fireplaces; we hadn't really done much to it, except simply restore it and repair it. We hadn't modernised it or changed anything, except for one thing. He suddenly said, 'you've changed it! That used to be a door', pointing to where there had been a door between the two rooms, front and back, which we'd actually enlarged to open up the space.

After that he just stood there and looked around. Then he said, 'OK. I'm going home now. I'm going home to my wife. She's 87 and I'm 89. She won't go out anymore, but when I'm in the area I always come round here.' We were curious, and asked 'well, where do you live?' 'Varden Street', he responded which is about three streets away. We were taken aback, as we thought he was going to say Chingford or Ilford or Billericay or somewhere like that. David Gold was his name, from a family of tailors.

◇ It's extraordinary the way memories can be instilled in buildings – and also how particular and local they are. Just three streets away was a different moment in time, a different world almost.

○ The East End had, and still has, although it's much less evident now, this amazing layered history, of all the various people who've lived and worked there at different times. When we moved to Whitechapel, it coincided with the beginning of the gentrification, which had started in Spitalfields. We couldn't afford to live in Spitalfields, but we got to know the people who were living there at that time. They tended to be people interested in the architecture of the place, because at that time it was pretty run down and dirty place to live; there were no smart schools and none of the bourgeois facilities that middle class people normally want. So, in a sense they turned inwards and began transforming their homes. There was a 'skip culture' where people would drag things out of skips and place them and create narratives in their homes.

And of course there were also the street markets of Brick Lane, Petticoat Lane, Club Row, Hoxton and Whitechapel wastes. All these markets were rich sources of artefacts, lots of items that the totters and stall holders had salvaged from derelict buildings. In Whitechapel there were whole streets of buildings that had been abandoned just waiting for demolition. It had never been done up since the eighteenth century – it had always been an area of decline. We are both from West London, where there's lots of Georgian architecture, which has gone through successive waves of being restored, so it lacks that original sense of mystery and history. The layering of history has been erased by these waves of renovation. But in Whitechapel, the economic decline that came at the end of the eighteenth century, when the area became full of sweatshops right until the early 1980s, in a way preserved the buildings. Some still had gas lighting and outside WCs.

◇ The slate was never wiped clean.

○ In a way it was a short step for us to the Soane Museum. We were making displays in our house of objects we'd found on the street or in street markets. Unlike at the Museum, these were very everyday items, basically rubbish, detritus, but combining it and putting it together in such a way that talked about a forgotten or ignored world and how important the ways of displaying things are, to how they are understood and interpreted. It's about how we relate to them, what they mean to us emotionally and how they affect our perceptions. So we started to make works that developed these ideas of display and presentation.

◇ It's a process of transformation which operates on two levels. It's about presenting an object and calling attention to it, giving it a different kind of status. It's not that it's necessarily elevating it, rather activating its histories and stories and meanings. And then, it's about putting an object in relation to other objects where one establishes networks and connections between them. Both are inherently creative acts.

○ We discovered that instantly when we were displaying a dried rat, a London stock brick, a dried-out cauliflower, objects that we found just lying in the street.

◇ Which, of course, also include your house which is itself also put on display.

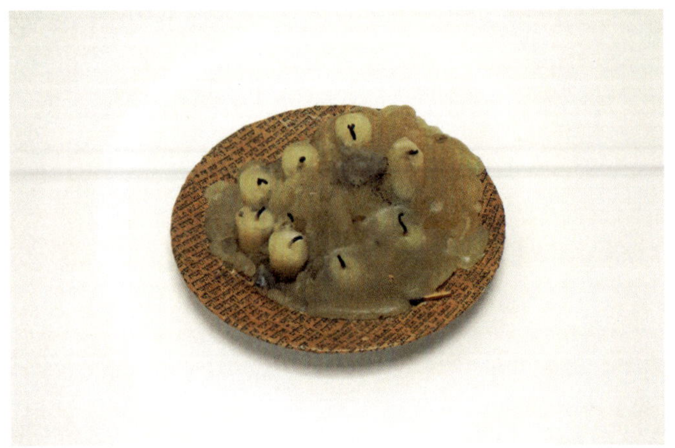

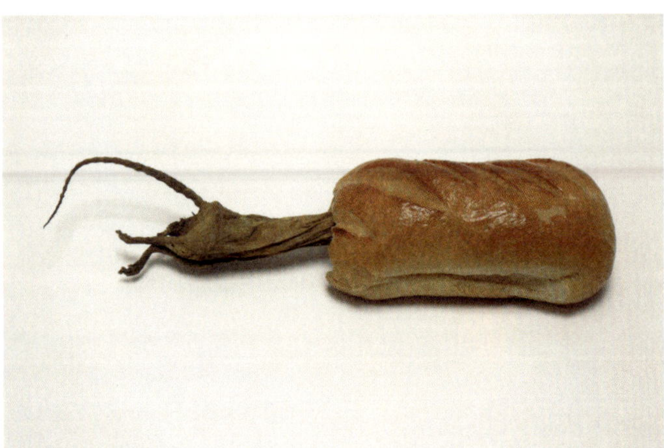

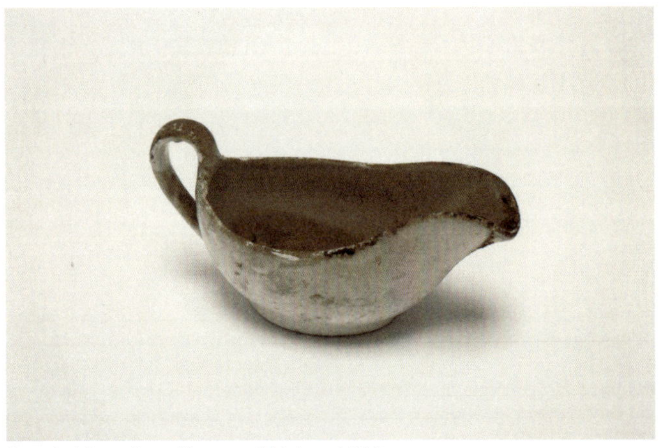

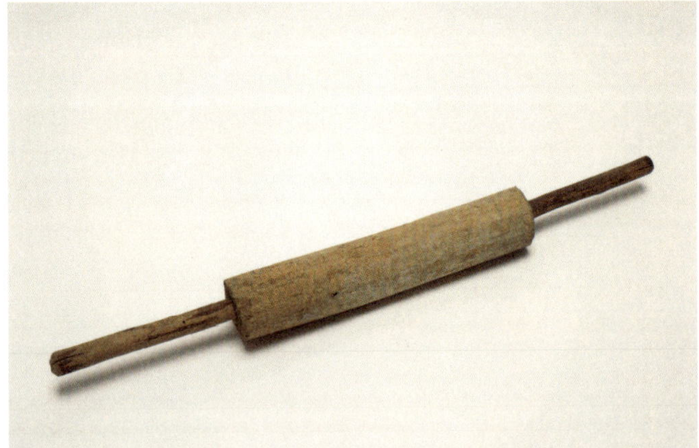

Found objects from **Traces of Living** 1986

Traces of Living installed at Interim Art, London, 1986

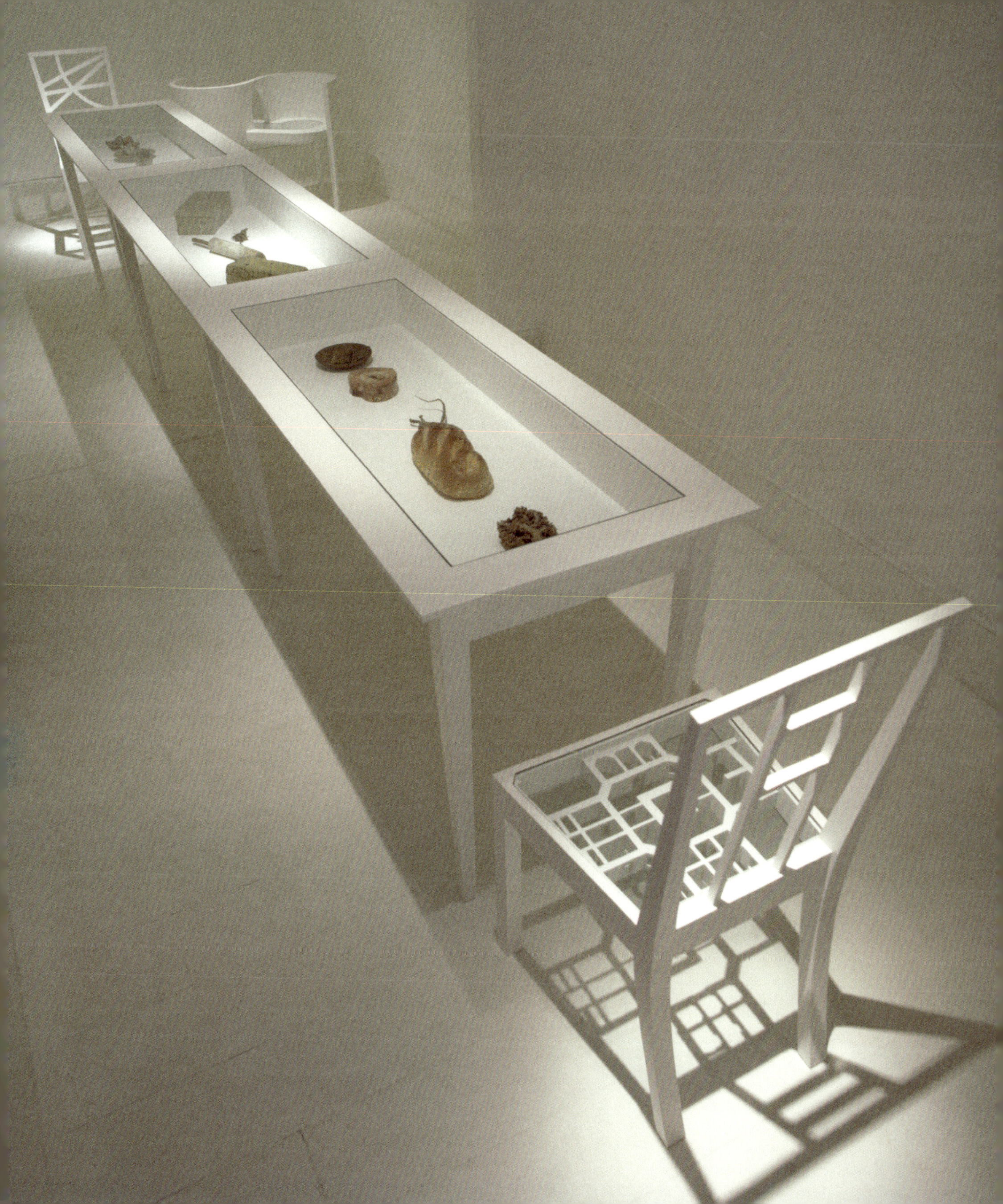

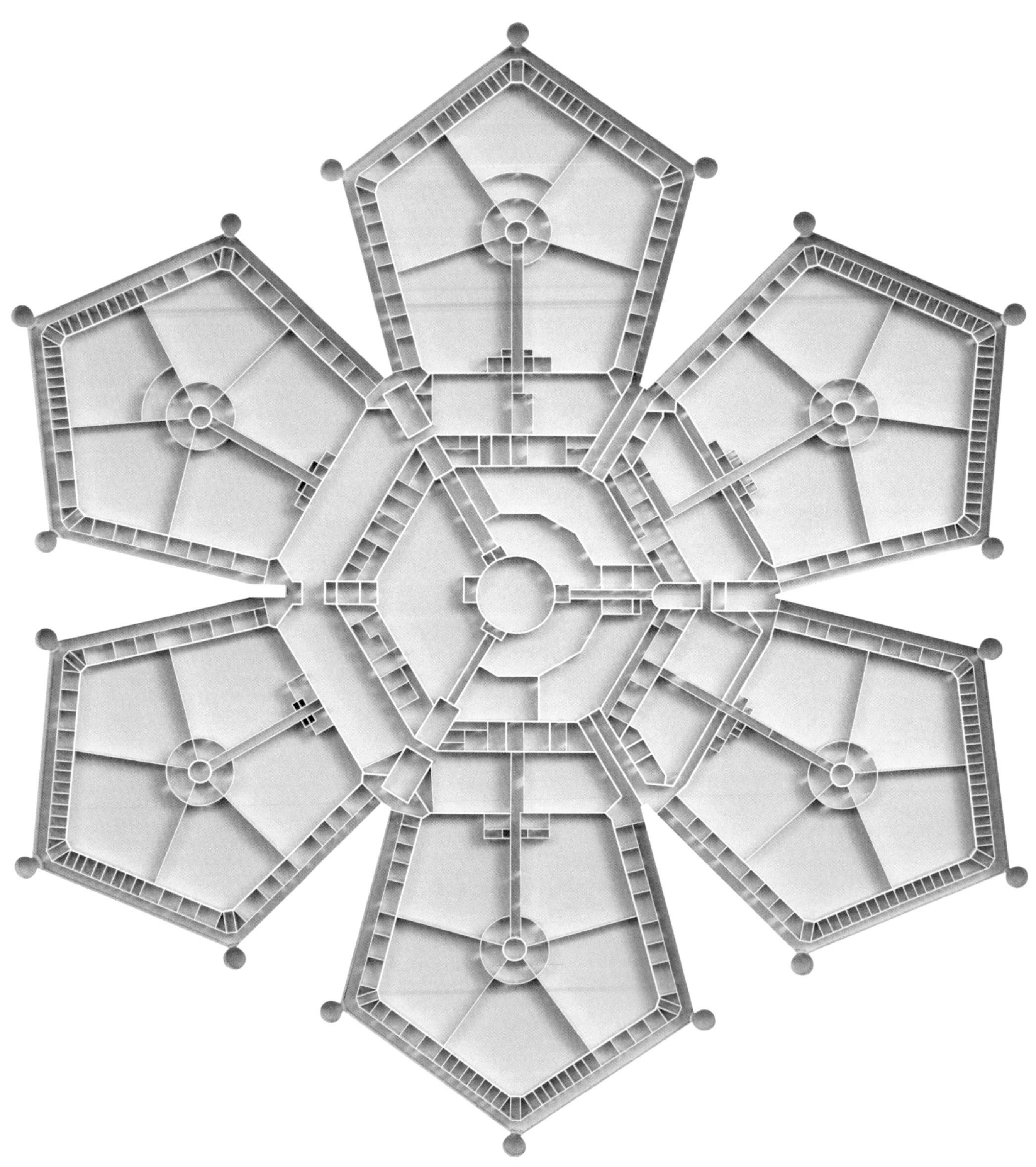

Surrounding time

◇ One way of looking at the architecture of the past is in terms of evidence. Every building one way or another contains the traces of its past users or inhabitants – your house in the East End made this point vividly. But at the same time there is a kind of parallel history in which buildings act as platforms or enablers for different types of activities.

○ Our work *Millbank Penitentiary* 1994 is particularly relevant with regard to this point. The building itself was actually erected on the site where Jeremy Bentham had proposed his prison – the Panopticon – should be built. The idea behind the Panopticon was that it was arranged so that all the prisoners could be observed by a single gaoler and would discipline themselves because they knew they could be being watched at any time. Millbank Penitentiary was a kind of bastardised version of the Panopticon, a building with a similarly radial plan, but instead of a guard at the centre it had the eye of God – in the form of a chapel.

What struck us about the building was its plan was so beautiful – it resembled a flower with radiating petals – but this was at the same time a reflection of its rather sinister purpose. Each 'petal' of the flower housed a different type of prisoner, murderers in one, petty felons in another, debtors, women and children, etc. in others. There was a paradox between the aesthetic purity of its plan and the fact that as a building it was all rational, about the will to control people through continual observation.

Anyhow, it didn't work as a prison and only stood for 80 years before being demolished and replaced by the Tate Gallery.

◇ Which is also about observation and control – though of a rather different kind.

○ We see galleries as temples of social and cultural aspiration. They exist to set standards to aspire to and to present things that we venerate, and in the process affirm social norms and values by which we live and order our society. A prison does it punitively, and an art gallery does it through what we elevate as high culture.

◇ Like prisons, galleries and museums are architecture at their most elemental: containers that are activated through rituals.

○ One of the first times we hung framed architectural models on the wall and displayed them almost like pictures was in our work *Museums in Motion* 1989. We chose three buildings to appear as the basic elements of architectural form: a square, a circle and a triangle. Bentham's Panopticon is the circle at

Millbank Penitentiary (detail) 1994

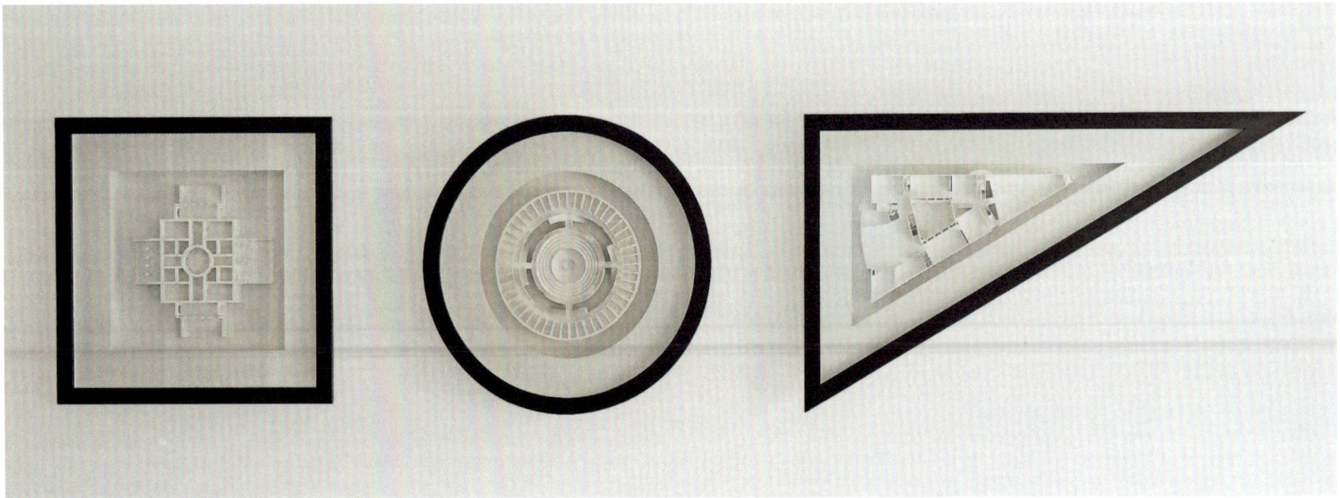

Museums in Motion 1989

the centre, which is the only time we've used a building that's never actually existed, as a subject for a model in our work.

In the lead up to making the work, we were looking at buildings, at plans, in a very direct, simple way and we discovered the Panopticon at about the same time we came across the plan for Palladio's Villa La Rotonda. We realised in some ways that they're the inverse of each other. With the Panopticon, the lines of sight are internalised. With the Villa La Rotonda, it's the reverse, everything is reaching out. In opposite ways, they're both images of a centralising authority.

The triangle is a much more contemporary building: MMK, the Museum of Modern Art in Frankfurt by Hans Hollein, which is also about looking and observation and surveillance. It was this very unusual shape because of the site on which it was constructed.

◇ Instead of trying to negate the shape of the site, Hollein instead emphasises and almost exaggerates it, rather like the other two examples.

All three have these very elemental geometric shapes which allowed us to combine the historical with the contemporary, and say something about the controlling nature of architecture. The Panopticon does this in a really explicit way, but in a sense all architecture conditions us subjectively by influencing our behaviour, our perception of ourselves, and of others. The Panopticon is

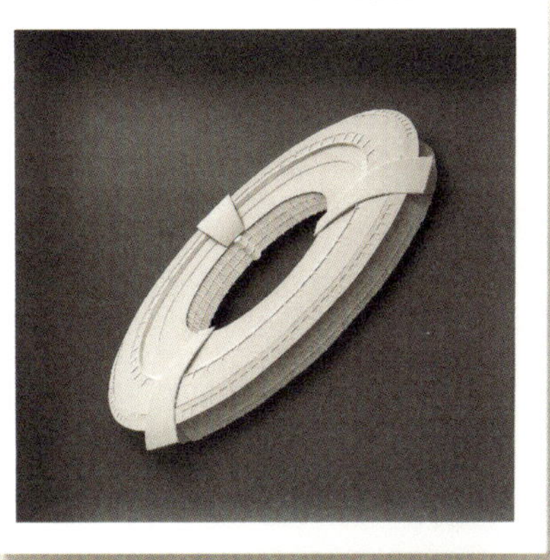
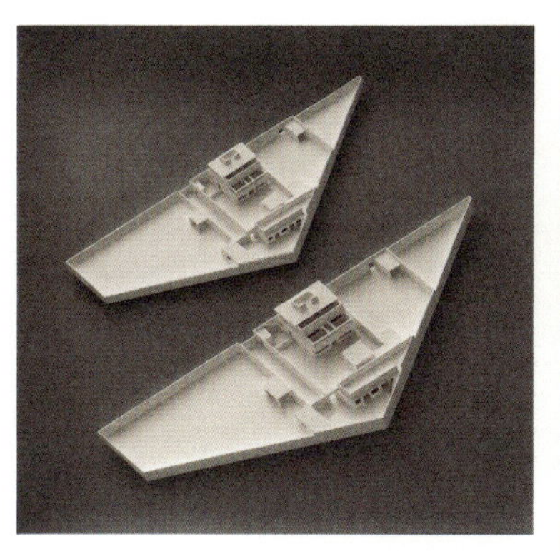
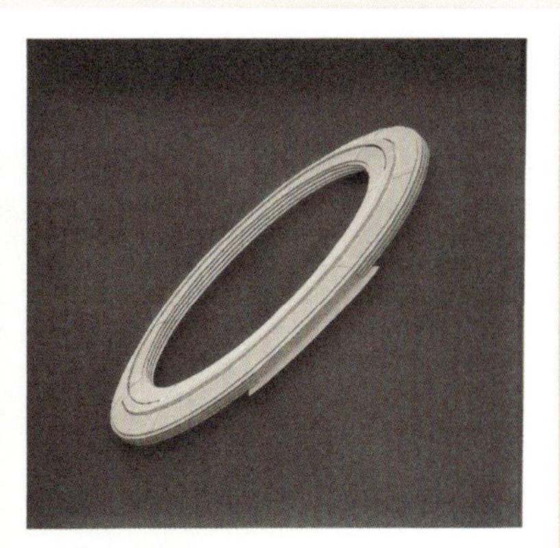

Infinite Loop 2014

predicated on this assumption; it was designed to control people's behaviour psychologically. It is one of the first occasions where a building was self-consciously designed with this direct purpose.

Museums in Motion relates through these ideas to another more recent triptych: *Infinite Loop*.

Yes, we made *Infinite Loop* in 2014. It combines a model of the last house of Osama bin Laden in Abbottabad in Pakistan with a model of the GCHQ building at Cheltenham, by Gensler, and a model of the new Apple headquarters in Cupertino by Foster + Partners.

The work began with our interest in bin Laden's house at Abbottabad. Because we had worked on one of bin Laden's previous houses, we felt we had a duty to record this house as well, as it was where he was discovered and killed. So, we made a model of it. At first, we had no thought for what we'd do with the model, but then we were suddenly invited to participate in the exhibition *What Models Can Do* at MGK, the museum of contemporary art in Siegen[1] in Germany, and we decided to make a new triptych.

We were very interested in the way bin Laden had been traced through his communications, so we began looking into the architecture of digital communication and were struck in particular by GCHQ and the new Apple building, and the way these Panopticon-like structures are connected through

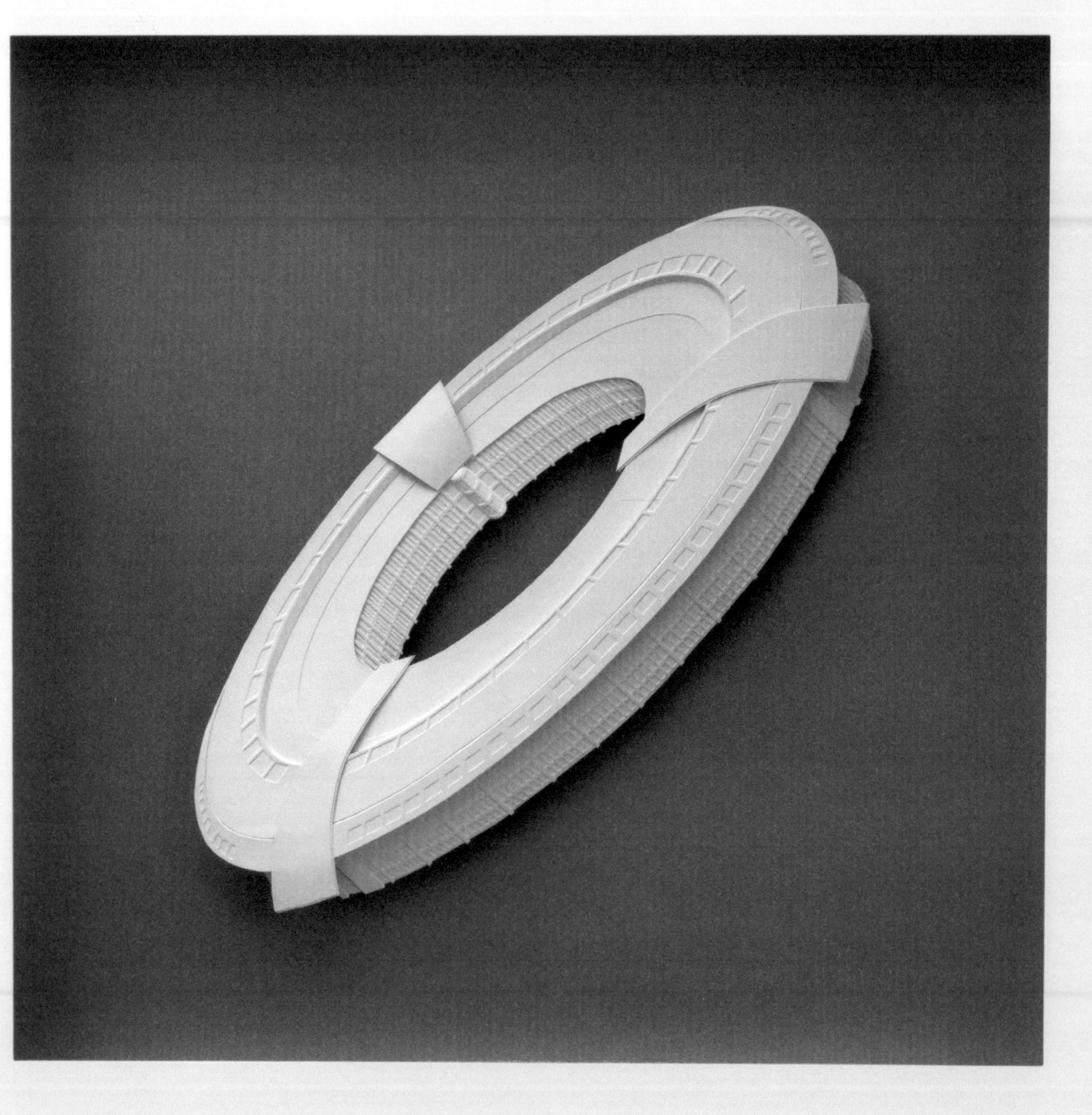

Infinite Loop (detail of GCHQ) 2014

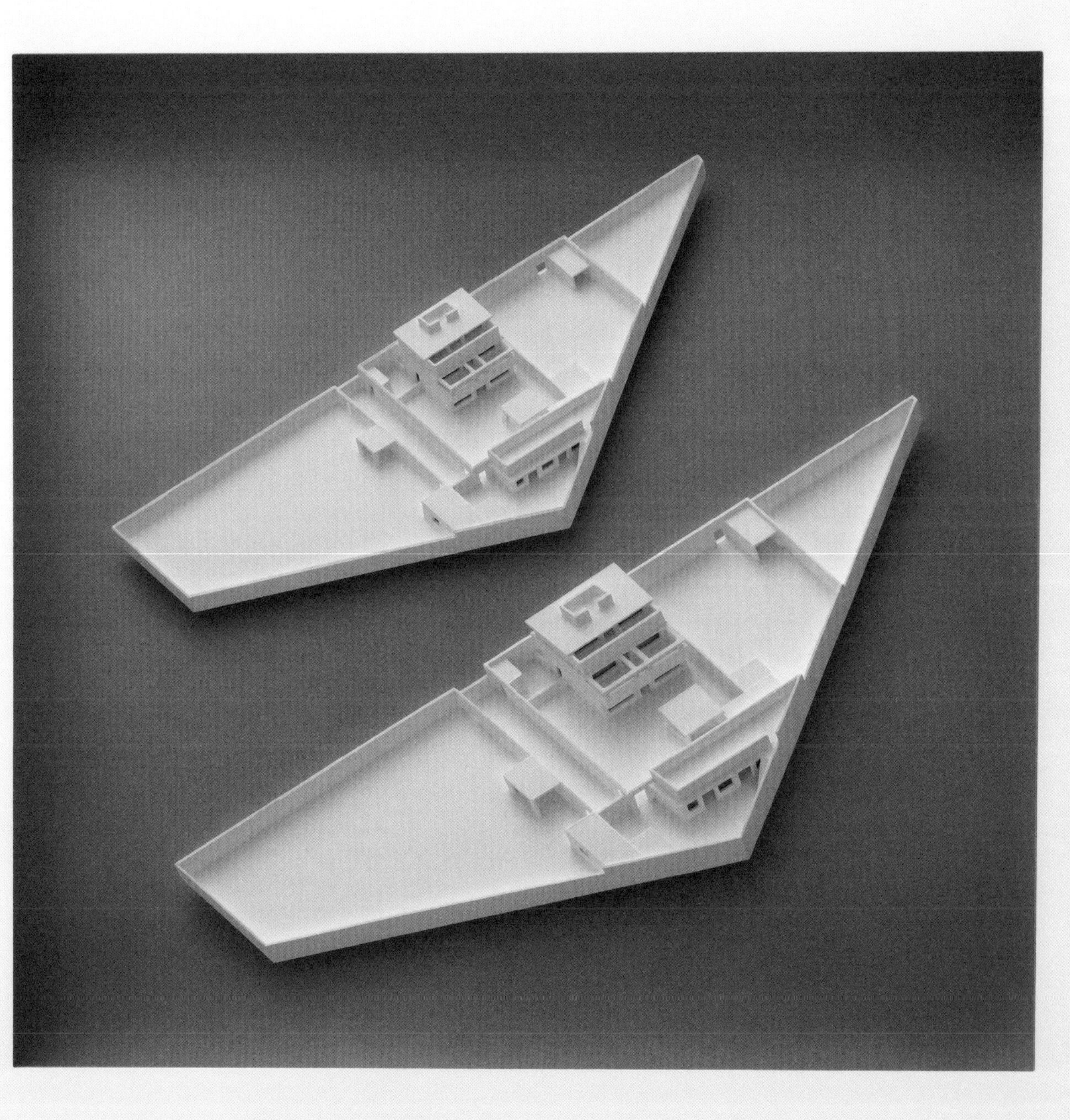

Infinite Loop (detail of the House of Osama bin Laden, Abbotabad) 2014

invisible digital networks. These and buildings like them constitute the architecture of the present age of super-surveillance, whether it's drones used by the military or Apple, Google and Facebook recording your every move, and heartbeat.

◇ It's not just Apple among the current big tech companies who have undertaken major architectural projects, all of them have been at it one way or another. On one level it's simply because these companies have grown so big so quickly that they all need more space. But at the same time their buildings are very obviously conceived as statements of the values, intent and aspirations of what are still incredibly young companies. Google was founded in 1998, Facebook only in 2004. This has been the focus of your recent body of work on the *Internet Giants*.

○ Yes, one of the things that struck us about Foster's design for Apple is that this big, circular, high-tech building embodies a very ancient typology in architecture. You see it in Stonehenge or in the Pantheon. It's a typology of spectacle, power and, today, corporate control and ambition. It's interesting to chart the lineage of a building like the Pantheon which had such an influence on the neo-classical architects of the Enlightenment, and on Bentham with the Panopticon. And then you have people around that time creating dioramas which then morph and mutate into cinema as a spectator experience, and to today's world of social media.

◇ I always wonder the extent to which the tech giants are conscious of the lineage of the typologies they are deploying. One of the striking things about Silicon Valley is the way all those companies function without any sense of history whatsoever. It's partly because they appear to be so relentlessly geared towards the future that there is very little self-criticism or even self-consciousness about the implications of what they do. They might feel all-powerful now, but history tells us it can all unravel incredibly quickly.

○ Somewhere deep within the psyche of these companies and their leaders there's probably a kind of nagging anxiety that the tech industry is very transient. Looking to history, there is this continual tendency for those in power to memorialise and monumentalise, to mark out territory through architecture, because they know power is fleeting.

◇ The typology is about imposing an order on an urban, or sometimes natural, environment – whether it's Versailles or the Pyramids – and thereby defining oneself against the disordered surrounding world.

○ Steve Jobs is definitely recorded as having ambitions for his building to last for a very long time. The Apple building is on such a vast scale – nearly a mile

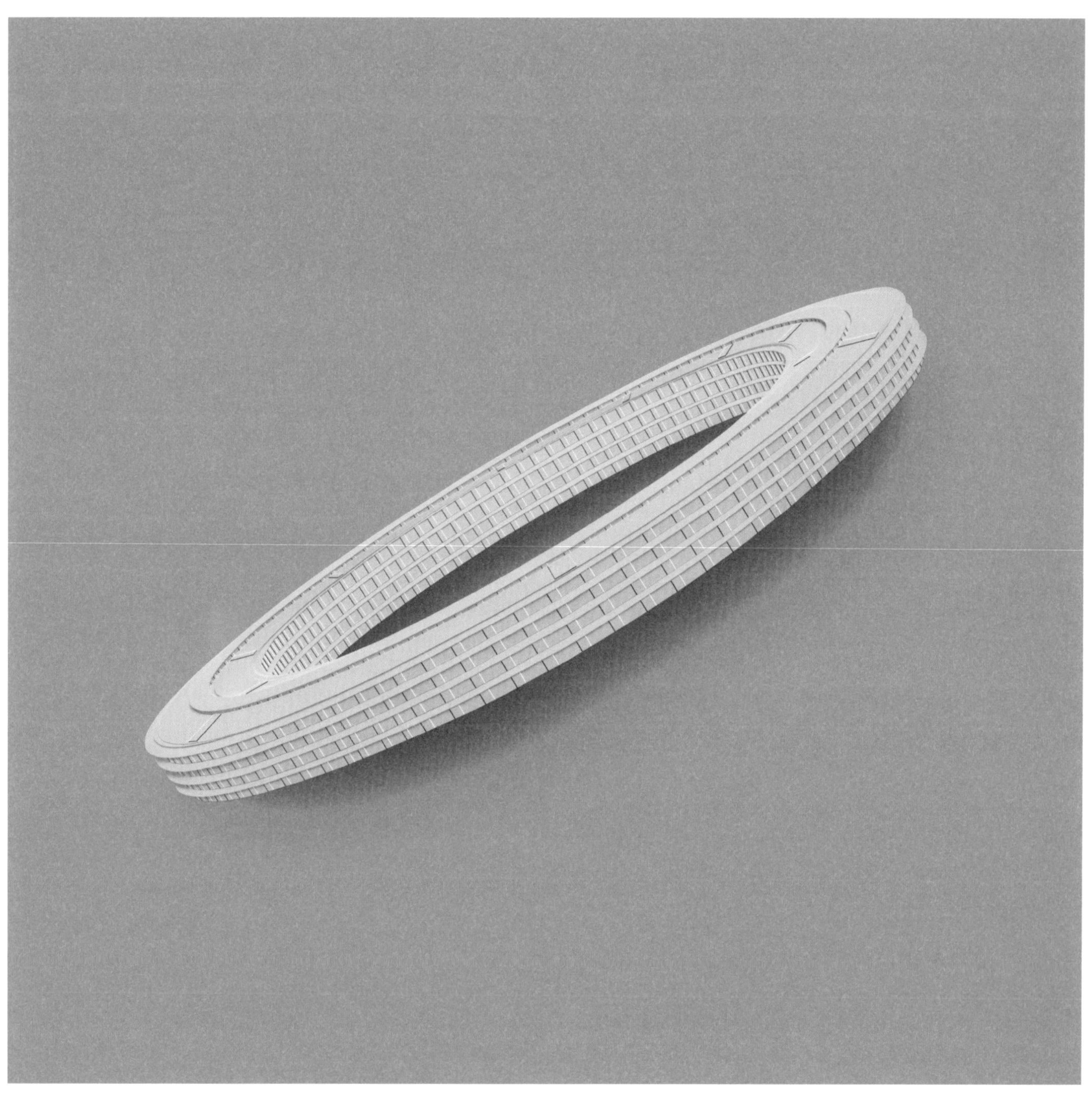

Apple Oblique (green) 2015

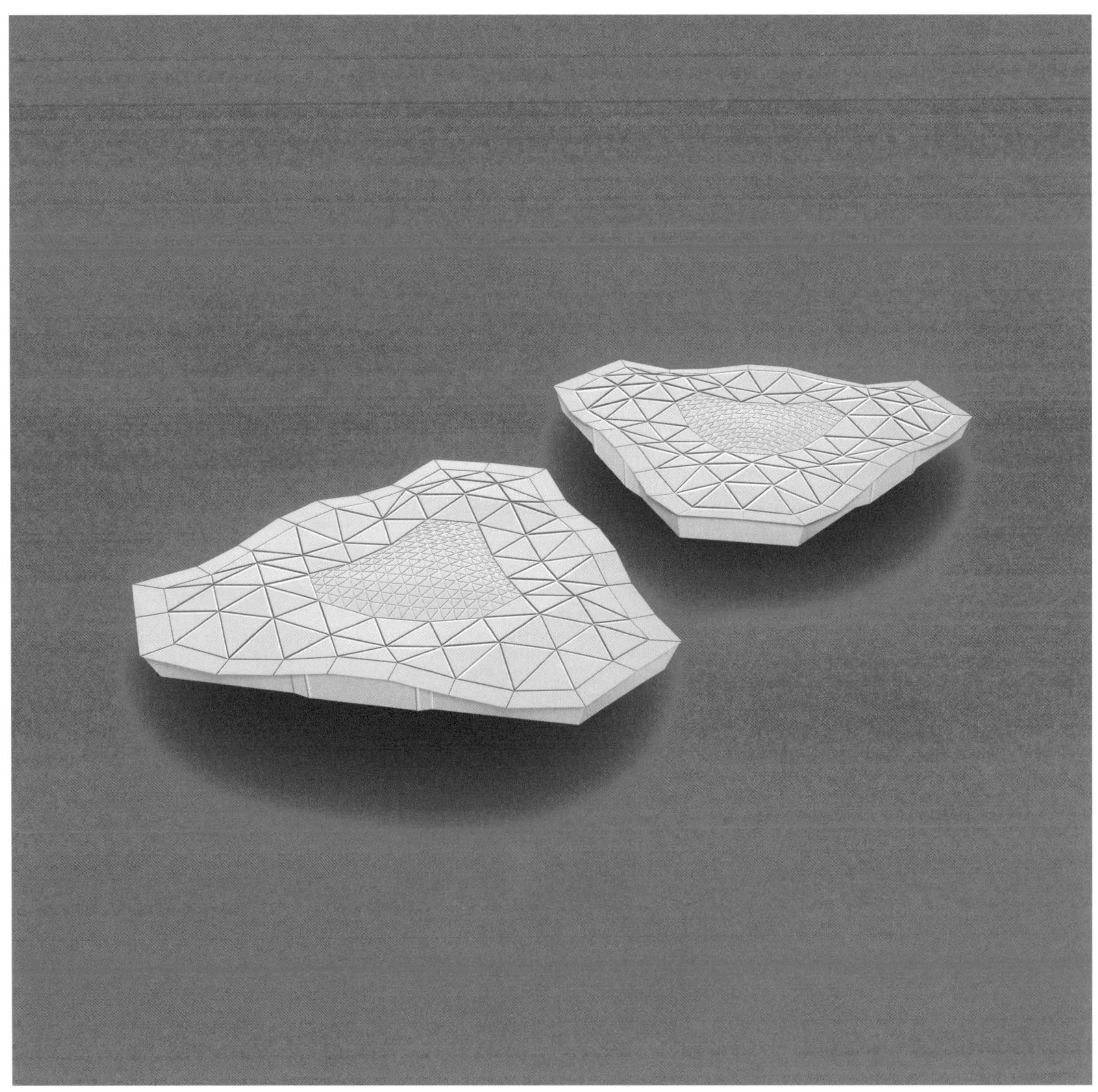

Nvidia, Santa Clara (orange) 2015

in circumference – built at such expense and designed by one of the most eminent architects around, that it might seem it has the best chance of any building to survive. Jobs was certainly aware of his own mortality and that was certainly figured in the building.

◇ He was almost living vicariously through the building. At the same time, it's hard not to see these buildings as huge decoys, not simply through their aspirations towards permanence, but because the most significant built – as opposed to architectural – imprint of all these companies are their data centres, which are located in remote locations where regulation is light and land and energy are cheap.

○ They're anti-statement buildings that barely reveal or demonstrate what they are in their architectural language. You just don't know what they are. Behind the façade you have no idea what's within.

◇ They're buildings that are designed to be mute, to obscure in a sense what is going on inside. They are conceived in entirely opposing terms to the corporate HQs which are the ultimate statement building – yet, as your work reveals, those statements are often misleading.

○ Our work is intended to bring these buildings into a clear focus, to treat them as objects, and to exclude extraneous detail or distractions. It's why we use the colour; it works to isolate them. It's a tactic that goes back to the *Logoworks* we made in 1990. These began through research into the plans of corporate HQs going up around that time in Frankfurt and other German cities. We used colour to articulate the plan as a kind of heraldic device so that it becomes almost like a logo.

◇ These works are fascinating because the transformation allows the plan to operate in two distinct worlds: the world of architecture, of which it remains part; and the very different world of the corporate logo. The work brings these two worlds – architecture and commerce – and their attendant discourses – into direct relation.

○ The thing with the *Logoworks* is that they are towers and the building is simply the extrusion of the plan upwards. You couldn't do the same thing with the *Internet Giants*. It wouldn't give you a real picture of the buildings, which are conceived much more like objects with spaces that flow into one another, that are intended to facilitate fluid movement and circulation. Comparing the two bodies of work, the differences are partly of function and location, but also reflect recent changes in design technologies and how corporations now portray themselves architecturally.

◇ Before the advent of modern architecture, this tended to be the task of the façade. Modernism made the plan the driver of an architectural project, with the façade, such as it still existed, a reflection of the building's function. So, it's very interesting when dealing with an emblematic work of the modern period, you focus on its façade.

You're referring to *Marseille, Cité Radieuse* 2001, which is a sculpture presenting a distorted view of the façade of Le Corbusier's Unité d'Habitation in Marseille. We made it from a photograph. We were actually staying in the Unité itself at the time and we took some photos of it from a very low, oblique angle, so the façade seems almost to be released from the normally rigid grid. From that viewpoint, it seems to jump into life, almost to take flight, so we were inspired to make a sculpture of it, which was followed by several others dealing with façades and interiors of other canonical modernist buildings. We made sculptures of the Bauhaus, of the church in Riola, Vergato in central Italy by Alvar Aalto, Le Corbusier's chapel at Ronchamp, and the Berlin version of the Unité, among others. The process remained broadly similar. We would make three-dimensional structures from well-known photographic views.

The fascinating thing about all of these buildings is that they became so well-known from photographs. It is mainly through the photographs that we experience them. These works reversed this logic by making a model from the photograph. In a sense, we're giving the building back some of it's original three-dimensionality.

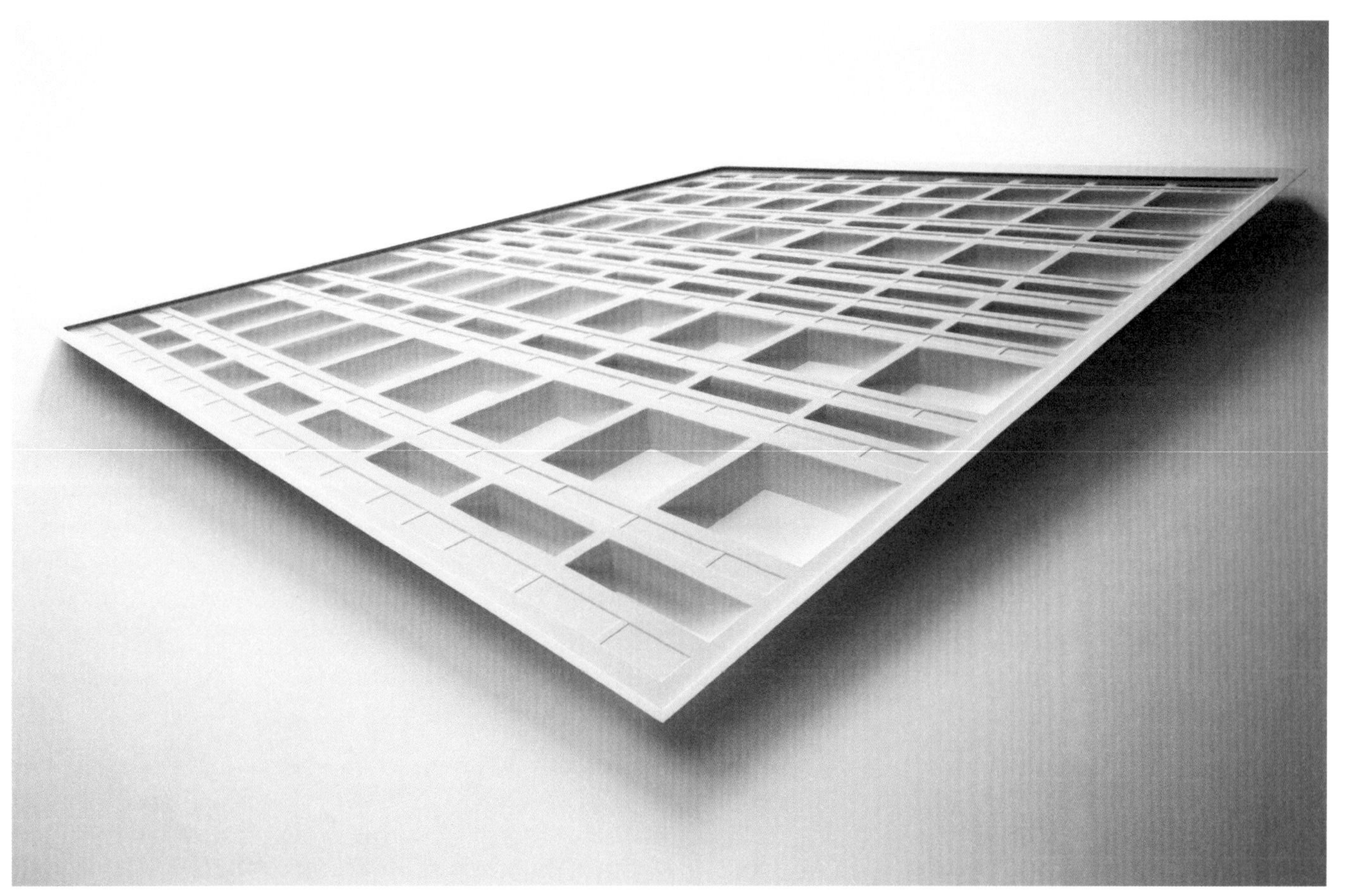

Marseille, Cité Radieuse 2001

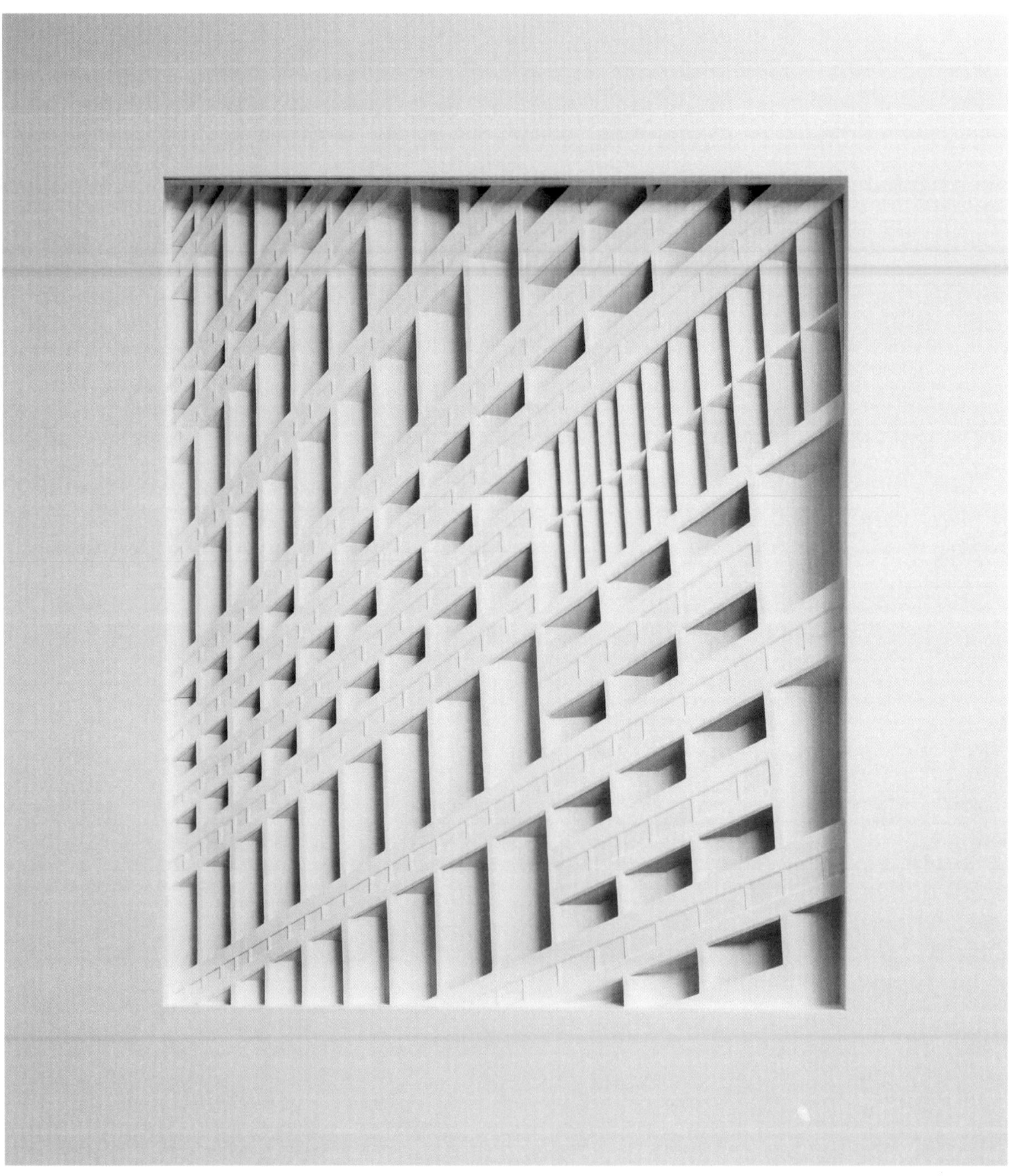

Façade Berlin 1999

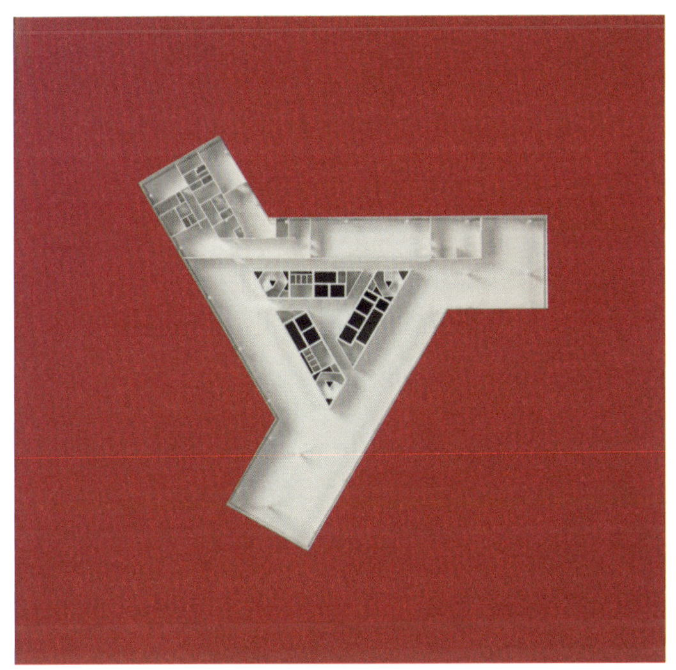

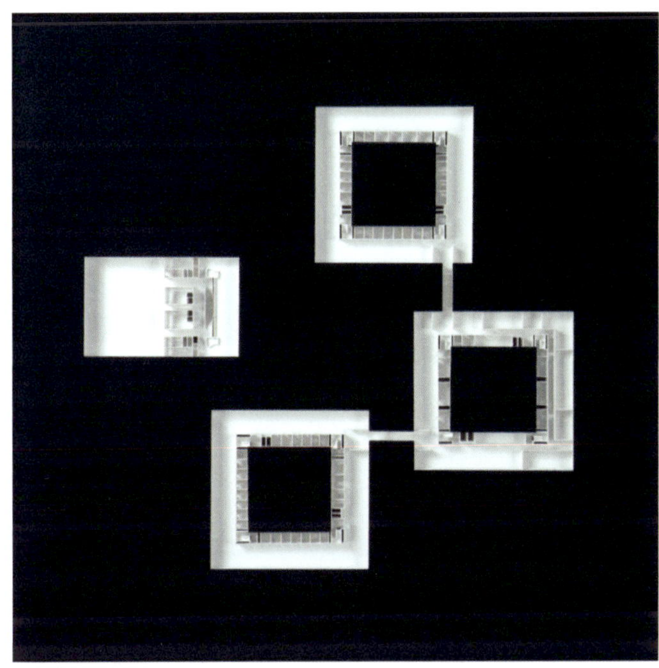

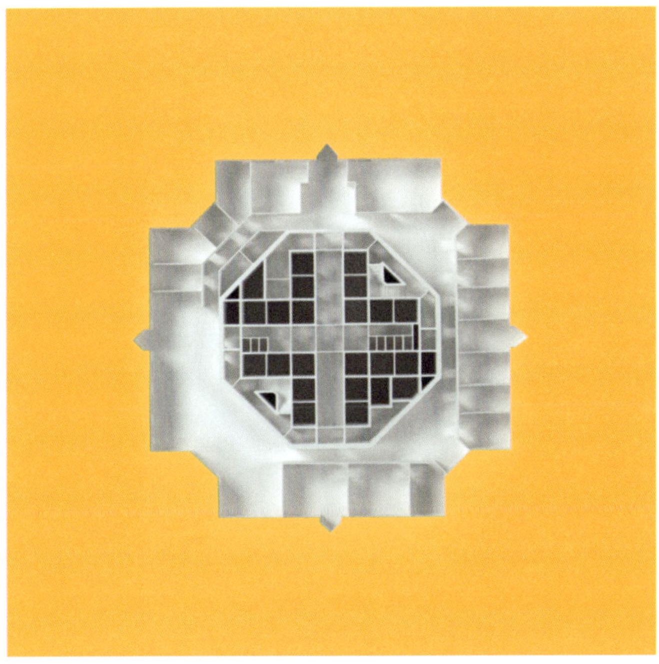

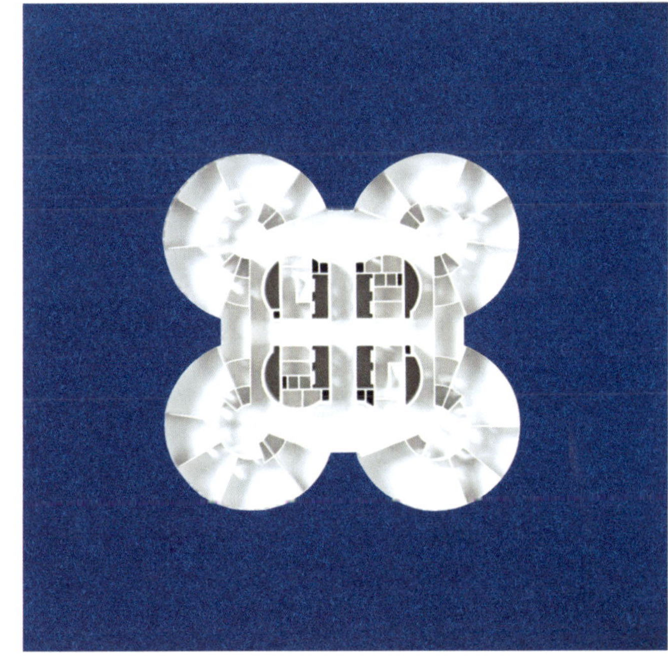

Logo Works 1998–99

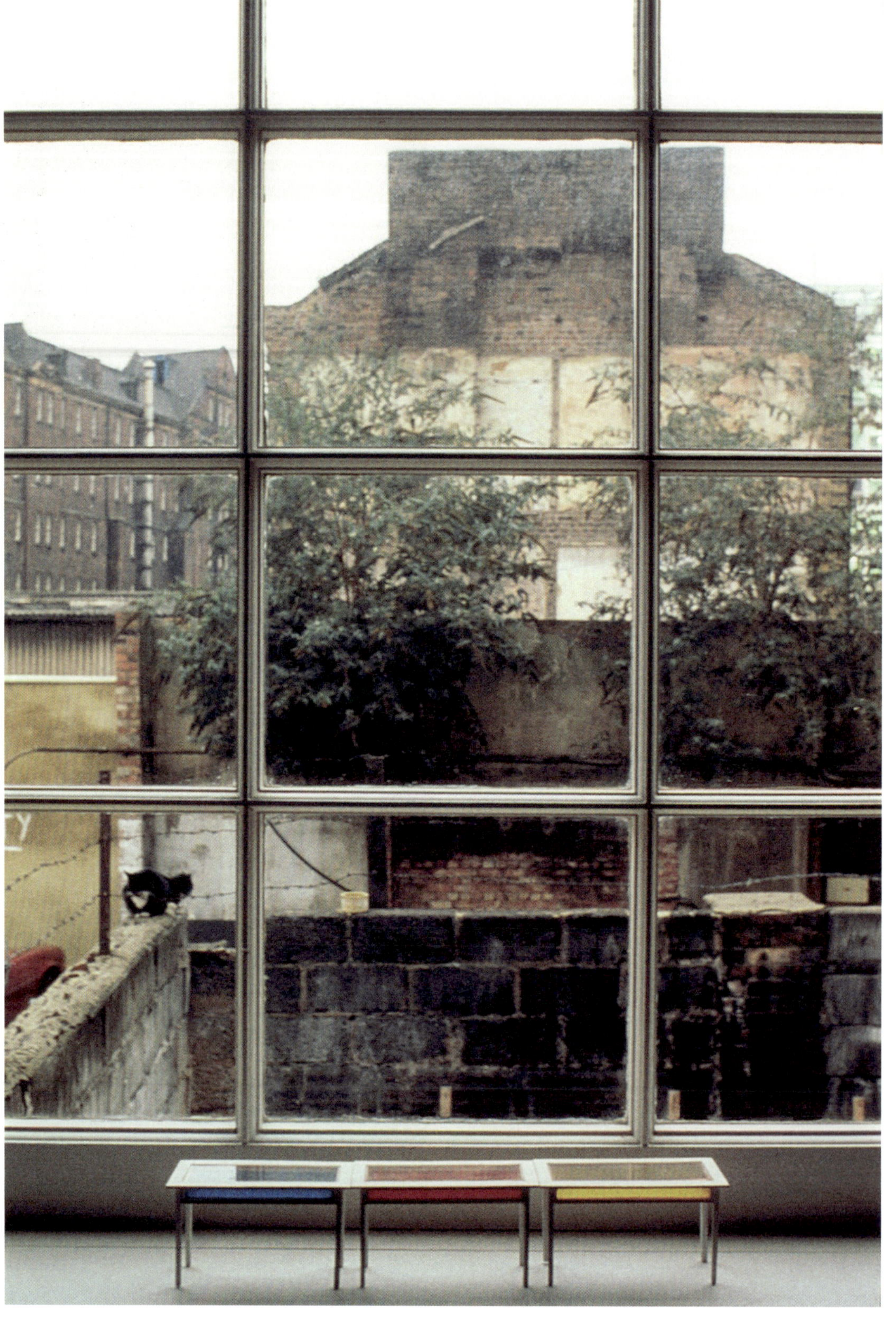

Degrees of evidence

◇ The idea of evidence – and its corollary truth – runs through your work. The title we have chosen for the exhibition relates to this enquiry, but at the same time appears to evoke a contradiction – truth is surely an absolute. But in the present moment of hyper-subjectivity the notion of truth that is something less than absolute is becoming ever more prevalent across the political spectrum.

○ Our work is ultimately about trying to make sense of our surroundings and of our encounters and relationships with people. It's about a way of looking at the way we live in the world and making sense of it. We are always discovering that there are so many clues in the simplest things about the way we live and about the environment that say so much about us and who we are. It's why we've homed in on architecture and interiors because they offer such strong evidence of the way we exist and the way we relate to each other.

◇ We've seen a proliferation of commentary describing how we have entered a 'post-truth' era, in part due to the tensions between the physical world and the online world of social media. In the latter we're able almost to find our own truth; or rather, we find it in what we are served up by algorithms. They seem to know us better than ourselves, predicting our wants, desires and political leanings. In the world of Google auto-complete, when truth is contained within massive data sets, we can legitimately ask whether free will as conceived since the Enlightenment still exists. In such a context, to create a work of art, it seems to me, is imbued inherently with a radical edge. The work is indisputably the thing itself, and inherent in it a kind of truth.

○ One of the things that motivates us to make art is that unless you make it, the world is incomplete. You're making it fit together. You're revealing things about the world that weren't visible before. And by making them visible, you're completing something.

◇ The artwork becomes a piece of evidence, at the very least of the moment of creativity that produced it, but also, hopefully, of something broader too. It's a crystallisation of a single moment.

○ In that sense, artworks are like buildings – they only come into existence at one point in time and then they acquire different uses, meanings and interpretations. That moment of crystallisation, as you call it, when a whole lot of different influences and trajectories come together remains the critical point; everything else issues from it.

◇ The moment of truth, so to speak.

○ It's linked to the fact that we always work with buildings that either exist or

Model for **Adjoining Rooms** 1989,
in Langlands & Bell's studio, Whitechapel, London, 1999

have existed. We don't work with buildings that we dream up or are fantasy notions. They're all actual buildings that have a specific identity, even if they no longer exist or are no longer used for the same purpose for which they were built.

◇ That's one of the fundamental differentiators between art and architecture. Both artwork and building emerge at an equivalent moment of crystallisation but their journeys begin to diverge almost from the beginning. Buildings are used, they wear, they are physically altered, they acquire new meanings quite independent to those they were originally imbued with.

○ We found that especially in our studio in Whitechapel that we discovered as a ruin. It has been many, many different things. It was a Christmas cracker factory, it was a stable, it was a synagogue, there was a fire there, it was a brush-maker's workshop, it was a belt factory, a stationery warehouse and now it's our studio. It has so many stories to tell.

There was even a famous murder there in 1874. A brush-maker, Henry Wainwright, murdered his mistress, Harriet Lane, in our building.

Wainwright had been having an affair and he didn't want his wife to find out. So, he installed Lane in a house in Bow. Unfortunately, she got bored and started drinking heavily, and her tongue started wagging. She began telling her friends about the affair she'd been having. Even though they had had two children together, Wainwright decided eventually that he had to do away with her. His brother became his accomplice, and together they lured Lane to his workshop on the pretence that he was going to give her more money.

Then, he whacked her over the head and killed her. He buried her under the floor, but he didn't put enough quicklime on the body to decompose her remains, and after a few months the smell became so bad that the neighbours began to ask about that terrible smell coming from Wainwright's building. So, thinking he was going to be discovered, he asked his brother to come and help him dig up the body, and they made parcels out of it to dispose of.

One of these parcels was carried out by an apprentice or someone working for them. The stench was so great that he tore open a corner and a dismembered hand was hanging out. As they called a cab on the Whitechapel road, the assistant realised that something dreadful was happening and they were obviously going to dispose of the body. So, he didn't go in the cab, but he followed with a policeman. They caught up with them on London Bridge just before they chucked the remnants into the water. The gruesome murder was revealed, Wainwright was tried and sent to Newgate Prison where he was hanged.

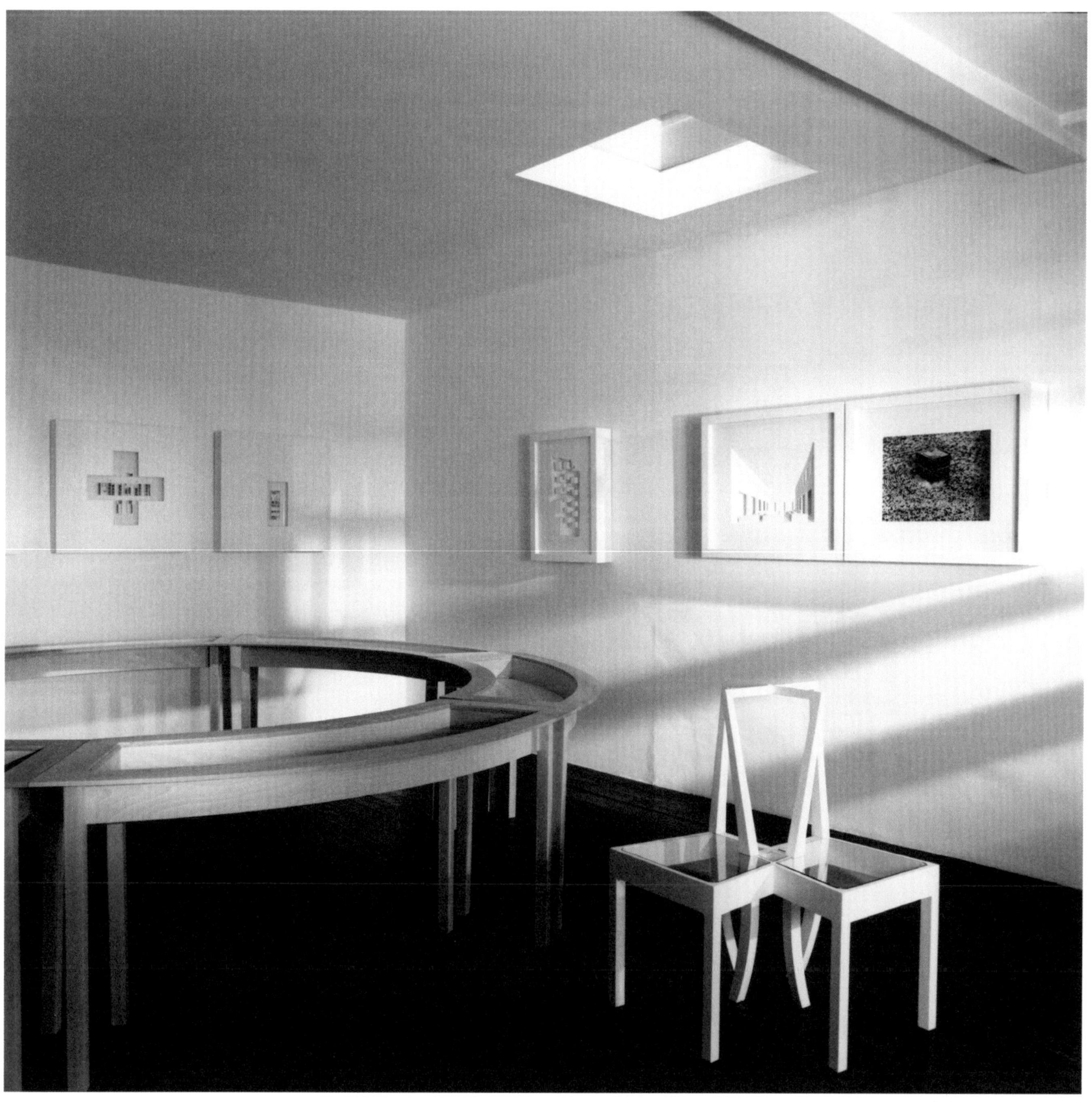

Langlands & Bell's studio, Whitechapel, London, 1996

So, buildings have many, many uses. They witness many things; you live and die in a building. There's this tradition in the East End where you are laid out at home after your death and people visit to pay their respects. It's quite reassuring actually to see somebody in a coffin with all their memories and photos around them; it's a way of passing on.

◇ Buildings have this capacity to carry truth that goes beyond simple evidence. It's a way the sometimes wholly immaterial traces of lives lived and events that have happened can somehow become startlingly present. I felt that with your work the *House of Osama bin Laden* 2003, a digital reconstruction of his house which you explore with a joystick.

○ We were commissioned to go to Afghanistan in 2002 to research the aftermath of 9/11 and the war in Afghanistan. Before we went we heard about bin Laden's house at Daruntah from a friend who had been in Afghanistan documenting the illegal girls' schools under the Taliban. We thought we'd try to visit if we could.

When we were in Kabul, we asked people about it, but nobody seemed to know anything. Then, one day we were on a journey to Bamyan, where the giant Buddhas were destroyed by the Taliban. We got talking to the guys we'd hired to take us there in a 4-wheel drive and it turned out that they came from a village near his house. We asked them about it and they said, 'yes, we know it well'. We thought it was empty but apparently it was being used as a base by the Hizb-i Islami, the Party of God, a local militia in the region. Fortunately, the drivers knew the commander and were happy to take us there, though warned us 'they're all armed'.

As soon as we arrived we took hundreds of pictures. We paced out the terrain, the compound and the buildings and made notes.

◇ What did this militia make of you?

○ They understood that because bin Laden had lived there that it was a notable site, and it still had strategic benefits, which was why they occupied it. And they realised why as Westerners we might want to visit and take some pictures. They also knew the dramatic potential of photographs with them holding Kalashnikovs, assault rifles and what have you. They wanted to be in all of our photos. We had to keep asking them to get out of the shots. They appear in our book waving their guns.

Anyway, they didn't like it when we got our tape measures out. They found it suspicious. We realised we had to leave quickly. We were a little bit naïve because anything could happen in that situation. We were lucky.

◇ What did you do with this material on your return?

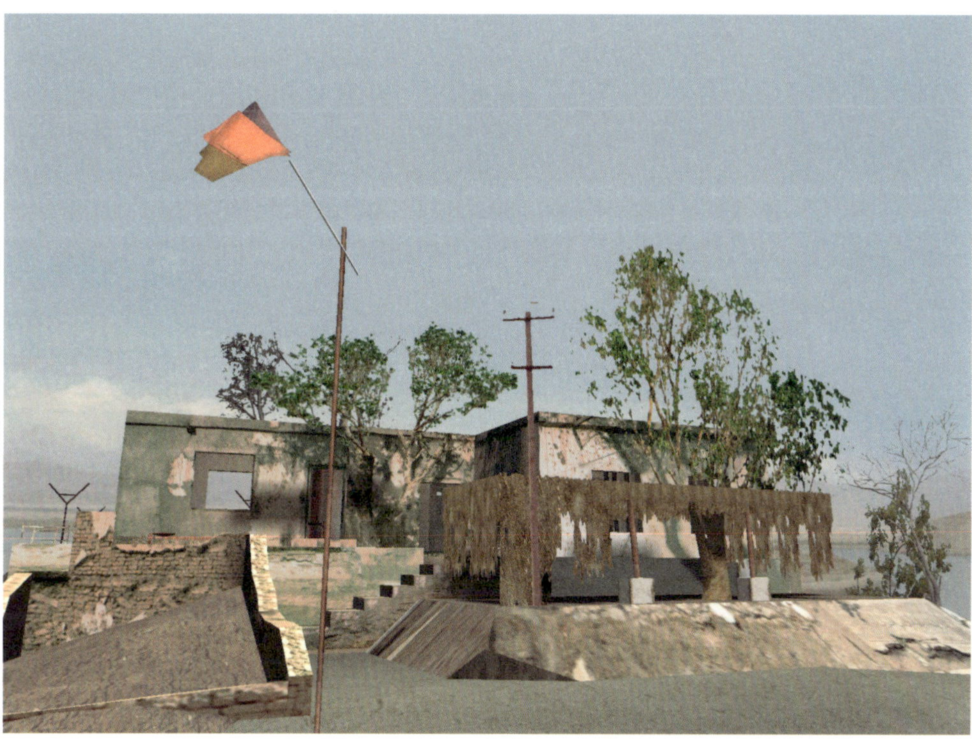

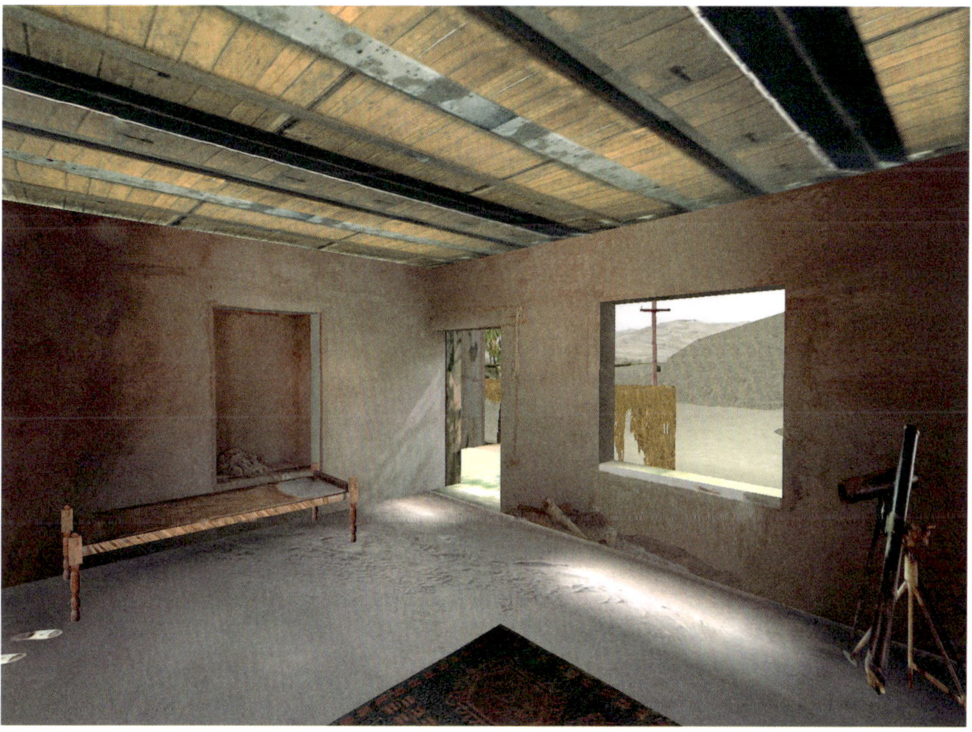

Screenshots from **The House of Osama bin Laden** 2003

○ When we came back to the UK we worked with an engineer to combine all the information to make a digital reconstruction, an interactive model of the house based on our measurements and using the photographs that we'd taken to texture the structures. The engineer had developed a system using the games engine from the computer game *Quake*, so that you could use a joystick to navigate the digital spaces we had built. You can travel around the house, move between different buildings in the terrain and explore the bunker. You can even see the mosque bin Laden built on the site.

But we've deliberately taken the aggression out of it. You're exploring architecturally his domain, but you don't actually find him – and unlike the game *Quake* you have no weapons.

◇ I wonder how this digital model relates to the physical models you frequently work with.

○ We think the technology we used for making *The House of Osama bin Laden* 2003 and *The Artists' Studio* 2002 was perfect for what we were trying to get across. In each case we were able to reconstruct a whole domain for people to explore virtually, as well as in their imaginations.

◇ The technology itself isn't neutral of course; it has its own meaning or set of associations.

○ Yes, we were highly aware that the technology we were using was very similar to the military technology used for targeting and training purposes. We were also aware that in a sense bin Laden was himself a kind of virtual presence. He is not in this domain we've constructed. He's elusive. At that time nobody knew where he was, or whether he was alive or dead. We thought this kind of technology, that exists somehow between fiction and non-fiction, was entirely appropriate to convey a figure who seemed at that point to exist mostly in the media.

◇ Since then, we have seen the rise of drones, which are operated from thousands of miles away almost as if they are in a computer game. The types of imagery we get from these conflicts plays such a large role in how we perceive them – whether it's the traditional 35mm photo reportage or the weirdly abstracted footage from satellites.

○ As far back as the first Gulf War when we made works like the *House of Arabs* 1990 and *Circular City* 1991, which were looking at buildings in Iraq, we were very conscious of the new types of videos you would see taken from planes flying at high altitude that were targeting structures tens of thousands of feet below. You would get these collapsed views at very compressed angles which now appear very typical of that time. We started making sculptures looking at

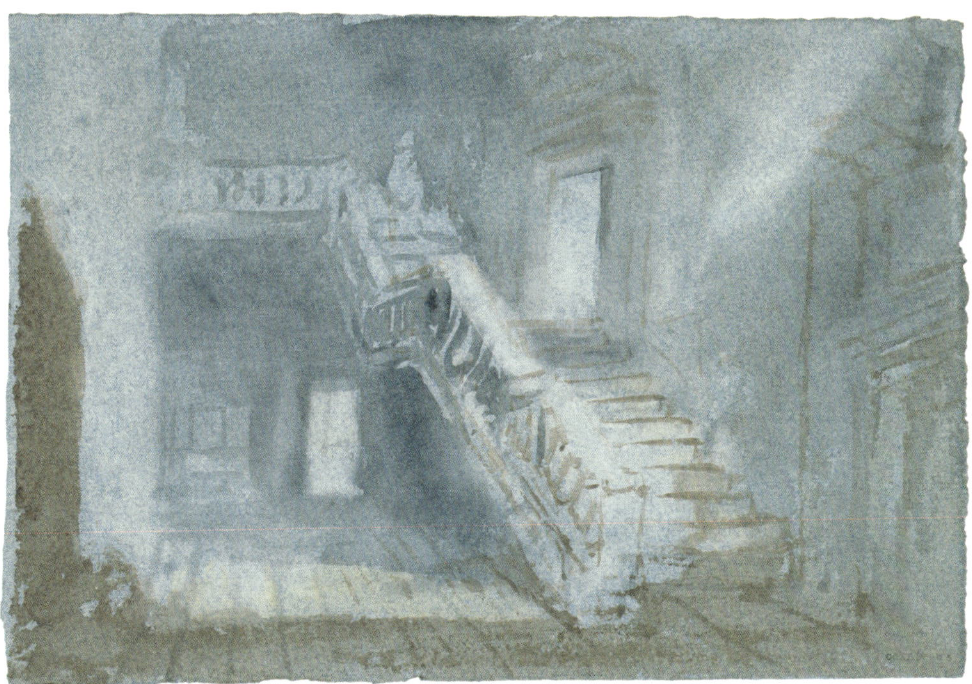

The Old Library Staircase, Joseph Mallord William Turner, 1827

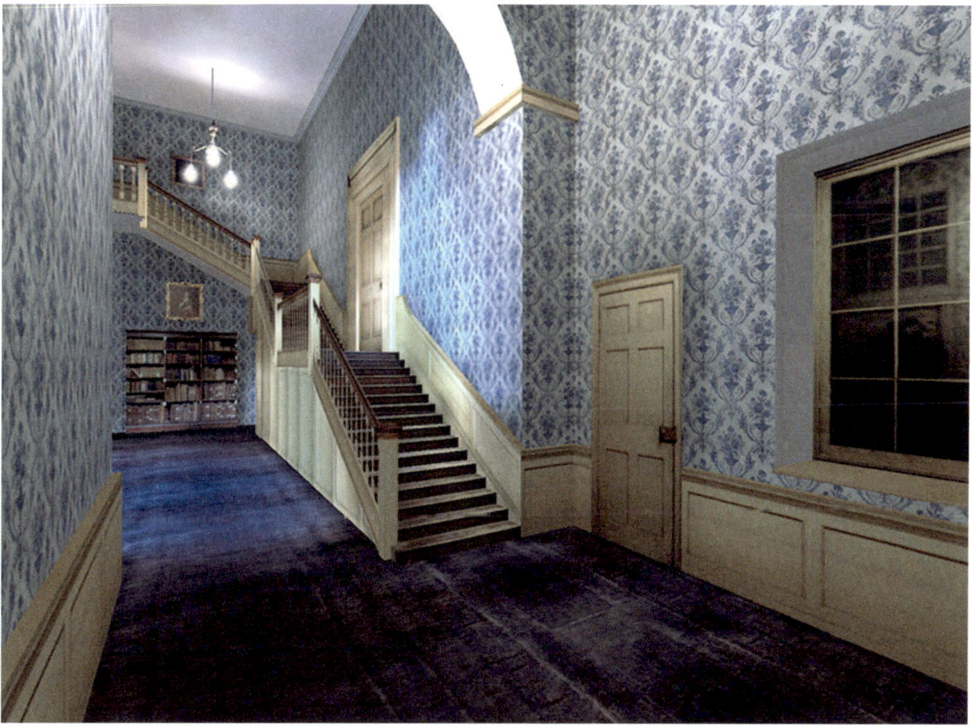

Screenshot from **The Artist's Studio** 2002

buildings with this very compressed viewpoint. However, in Afghanistan, technology had moved on, so you got views from drones that read as digital simulations.

◇ Even though the footage gathered from these technologies looks and feels quite different, the viewpoint always remains the same, looking down from a safe distance – literally and metaphorically. It's rare to see things from the perspective of those on the ground, which is another reason why *The House of Osama bin Laden* is so powerful and arresting.

○ Interestingly when we were at bin Laden's house, several Black Hawk helicopters flew over and we took a photograph that we subsequently made a work from – so we have that piece of evidence as well.

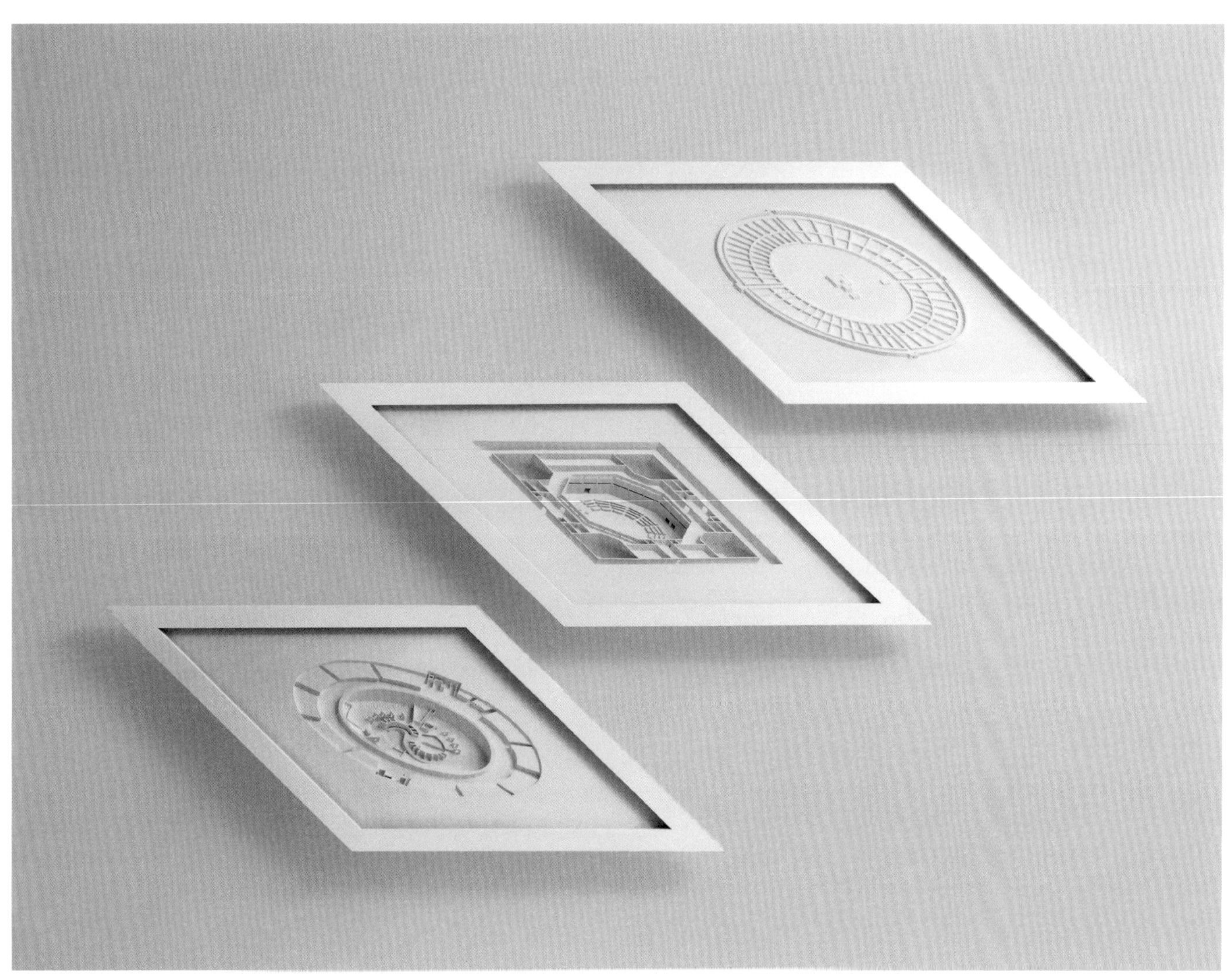

House of Arabs 1990
Wood, paint, glass, lacquer; 180 × 220 × 15 cm; Saatchi Collection London

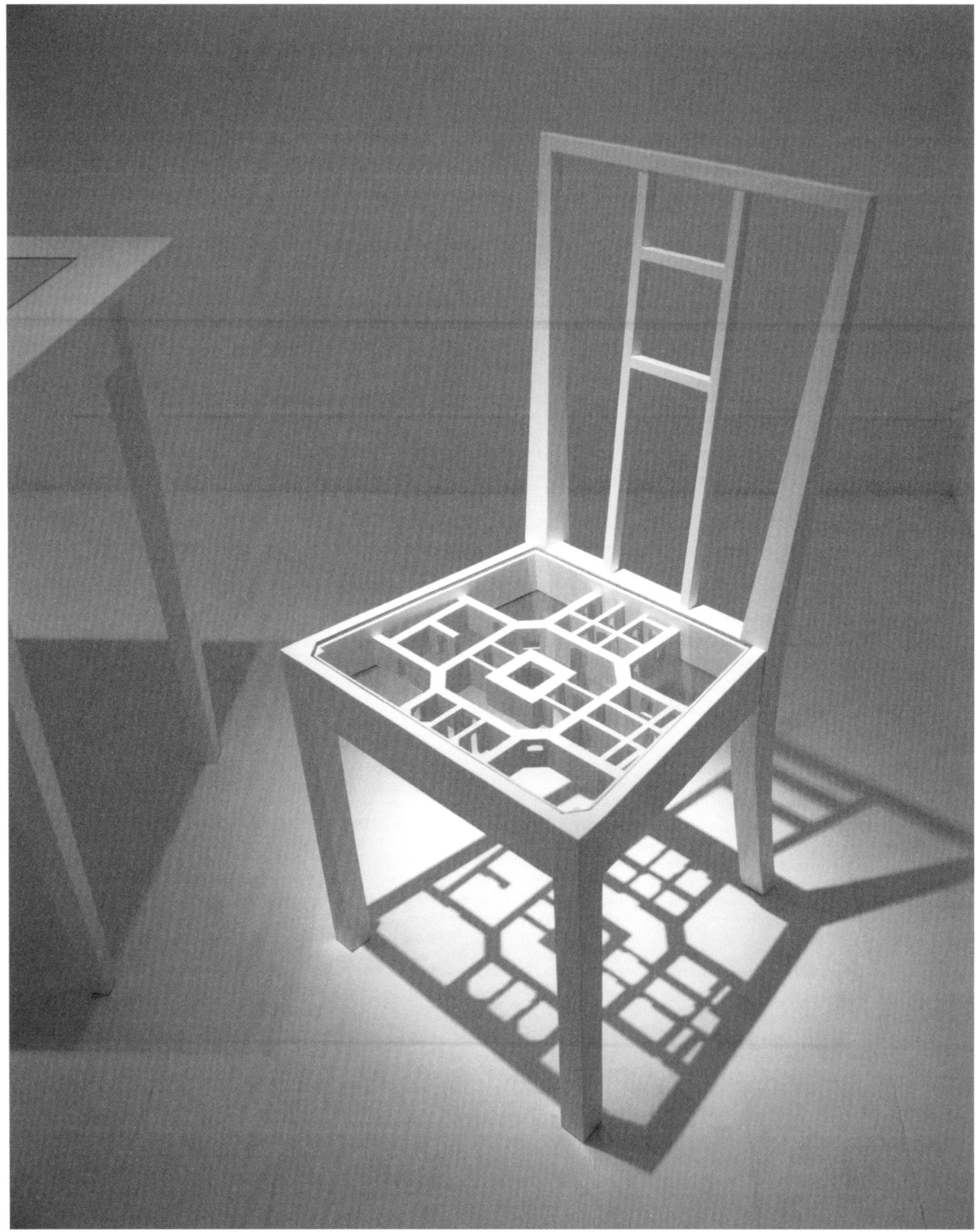

Traces of Living, Interim Art, London, 1986

Transforming objects

○ When we first showed *Traces of Living* in 1986 at Interim Art, Maureen Paley's gallery in her house in Beck Road, one of the objects we displayed in the tables was a single yellow stock brick.

◇ Where had the brick come from?

○ Somewhere around there; we can't remember precisely. There were lots of building sites and still many bomb sites, even in the early 1980s.

◇ So, it could have been any brick?

○ Yes, for us, it's what the brick points to, what it symbolises. After all most of London is built from either red brick or yellow stock brick. By placing an object like that under glass you're creating a greater scrutiny. You're elevating it in a sense, allowing people to look at it in another way. They wouldn't look twice at those objects normally, but by placing it in a beautiful white display and under glass you make people take notice.

◇ In the context of the Soane Museum the brick has a further meaning, because Soane was the son of a bricklayer. That legacy stayed with him, both through the fact that throughout his life he was seemingly very conscious of his comparatively lowly social origin, and the almost instinctive feel he had for building materials. It's interesting how the brick acquires these meanings in relation to the setting in which it is placed – its spaces, objects and stories.

○ You're also making connections between different objects and the ideas and associations they conjure. You're saying that these things belong together and you're creating a narrative. By selecting them you're elevating them and by combining them you're making links between them. In the art world these things are called 'found objects' or 'assisted objects', but for us they're more than that.

◇ Initially at least it's important that you were displaying these objects more or less where they were 'found'.

○ Yes, in the early 1980s we were working with ideas of architecture and furniture and also making artists' books exploring connections between books and architecture. Bricks are modular units that can be accumulated ultimately to build a house or city, and words similarly are modular units from which you can build language and write books. We made a work called *The Ruined Book*, 1982 which was a two-metre-high sculpture of a book made from plywood. We covered it with that kind of brick wallpaper that you used to get in decorating shops as a bit of kitsch fancy to cover your chimney breast or something like that.

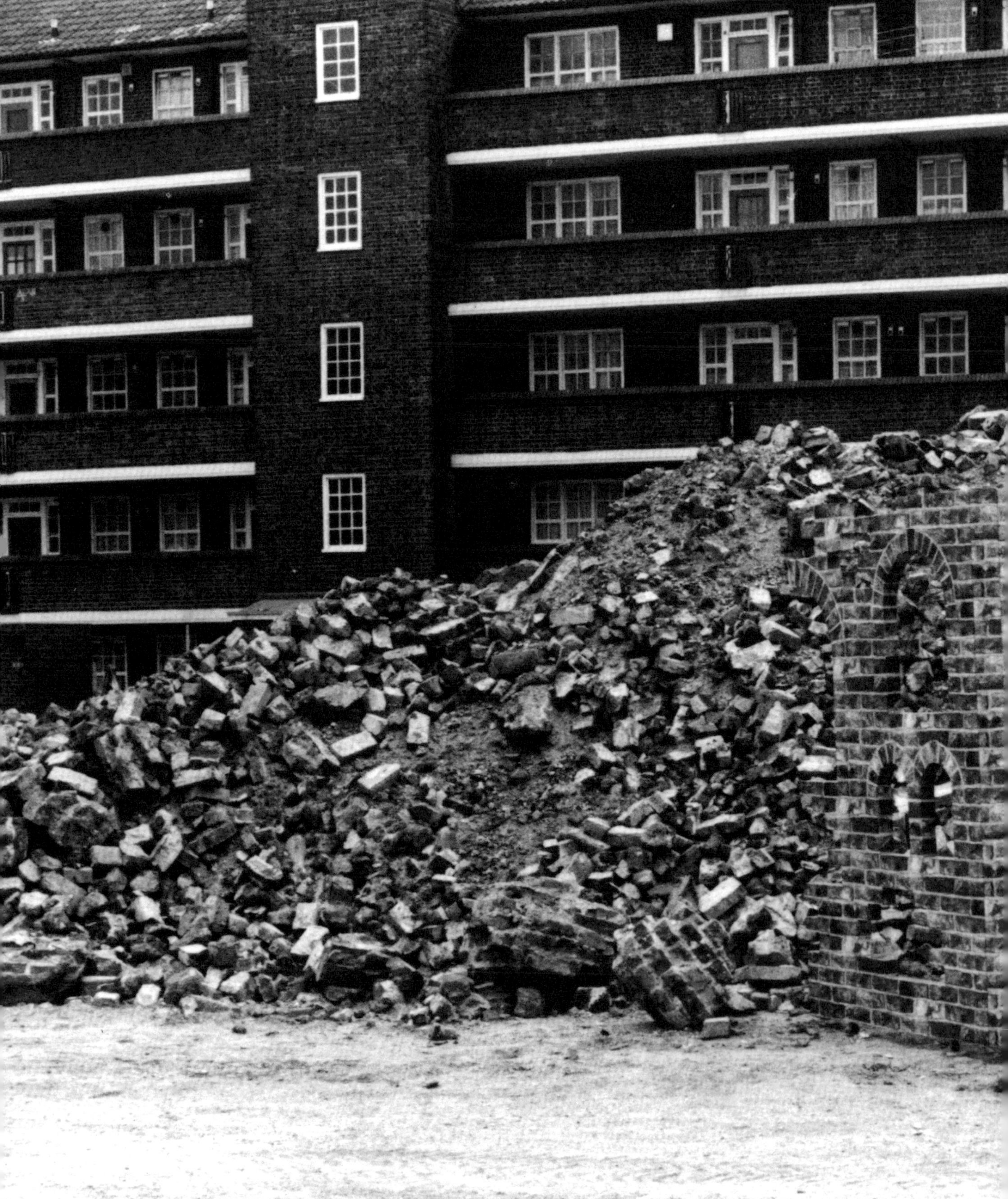

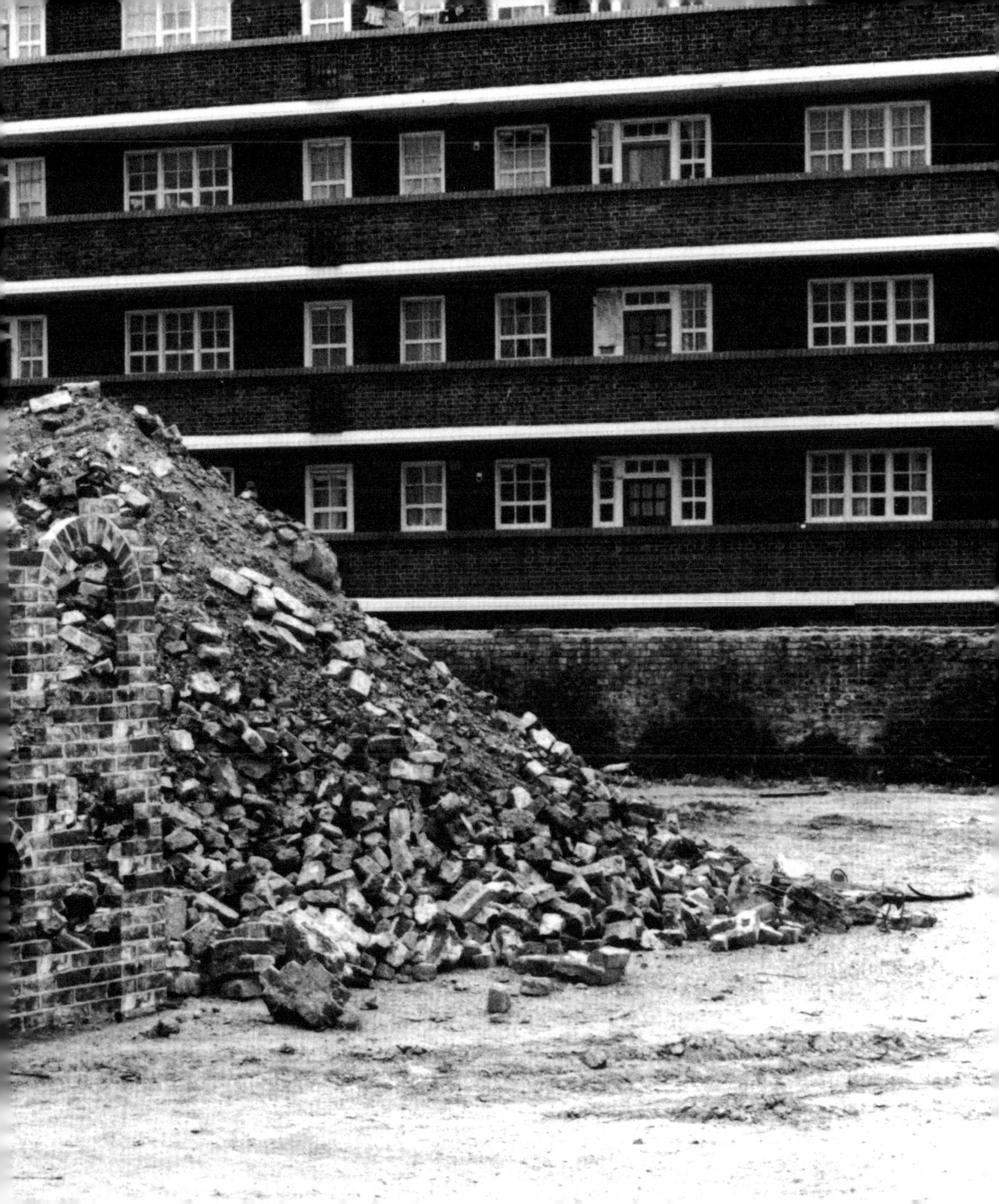

Previous pages
The Ruined Book,
Wapping, London, 1982

Once we'd made the sculpture we decided to take it down to Wapping where they were demolishing some 1930s deck-access blocks of flats. The area was undergoing a transformation. The beautiful eighteenth- and nineteenth-century wharves were just starting to be converted into what were then known as yuppie homes. But those deck-access blocks were very un-loved, and were making way for new developments. It was the beginning of gentrification.

We took this sculpture down on the roof of our Mini, and we stood it in front of the pile of rubble from the demolition and photographed it in black and white. When we saw the photographs we were amazed how the sculpture just blended into the surrounding rubble like it was camouflaged. It became a ghostly structure resembling both a book and a fragment of a ruined building.

Afterwards we destroyed the sculpture; the photograph is the evidence. It's a pivotal artwork for us.

◇ Again the setting was crucial, anywhere else and the meanings are quite different.

○ Yes, we were exploring London architecture as a kind of social aesthetic history. Looking back, it was then a fairly short step to start making sculpture that took the form of furniture and models of buildings. In those works we were similarly treating furniture and even buildings themselves as 'found objects'. By re-making buildings as models, we were able to take something that existed on the scale of the city and transform it into something containable that could be very specific.

◇ One of the first models you made was of the National Gallery.

○ At the time we were making money by making furniture and restoring houses for people. We met this architect, and he said 'I need a model maker, and I think you could do it. Will you have a go?' Luckily, we had taught ourselves to read architectural drawings, so we thought we could manage it. The architect worked for the Property Services Agency – a now defunct body that maintained government buildings. Apparently, they wanted to fit air conditioning in the basement of the National Gallery, and they needed a model in order to work out where to route the ducting and the plant. We made the model to come apart in different ways so they could analyse where to put things. It was a great education in the art of model-making. We kept the drawing they gave us and used it to make our own model which we put into the seat of a chair.

◇ With the result being to transform the status and meaning of not just the model, but the chair, also. It's interesting that it was the basement of the National Gallery, the private space of a public building.

○ It was important to us that we weren't talking about the grand galleries of the National Gallery, or the imposing façade, we were talking about the basement where work is stored and the public never visits. But it was vital to us that it was indisputably the National Gallery; that it wasn't just any old building.

By placing the model into the seat of the chair, the work was saying that furniture and architecture belong together, that they reflect on each other, and they modify each other. And to use a postmodern term, you can begin to decode architecture by looking at the furniture within it.

Furniture describes or evidences how we use buildings. It mediates between our bodies and the building. It enables our activities within buildings. It's the common denominator in a building, something everyone uses and relates to. And in that way it indicates a person. It's a token or a sign of an individual or of the group. Without needing to get into representing people figuratively, furniture implies their presence or their absence, their activities and their relationships whether personal or political, economic or technological.

◇ In all of your furniture works, your chairs especially, the crystallising moment is when you place a model or an object into it and it is transformed from an everyday functional object into an artwork. When it's the National Gallery, and specifically its basement, it invokes all those ideas and debates about cultural hierarchy, the canon, and fundamentally the relationship between the artwork and everyday life and the role of the artist in mediating that. It's a constant thread in your work.

○ It reminds us of another 'found object' that became an artwork. Years ago we used to make lots of forays into Brick Lane to an extraordinary market where people would hold up one shoe with a shoelace, and that was the only thing on their stall.

We were wandering along early one Sunday morning and went past a stall where the only thing on it was a filthy piece of plastic with an old couple leaning over it. We were curious and asked, 'what's this?' They responded, 'we don't know what it is', so we peeled back the cellophane and there was an extraordinary wind-dried carcass. It was like an Egyptian mummy. It had all of its whiskers intact and its teeth and the tail and it had a notice in its mouth in wobbly writing, saying 'please do not feed'.

Intrigued, we asked, '*how much* is it?' '£5' was the answer, but we only had £5 on us, and we didn't want to spend it all on one thing because we were just starting to go through the market. 'We'll have a think about it and we'll come back', we said.

We carried on up the market, and bought a few things that we needed. And, of course, we came back to it because we thought it was such an odd thing. They were still there; they hadn't sold it. So, we said, 'will you accept £3 for it?'

and they said 'oh, all right then'. And we bought it for £3.

As we carried this strange wind-dried creature up the road, a gaggle of East Enders came around us and said 'that's a whippet, that is. That's an East End racing dog.'

It made sense, because there's a tradition of racing whippets in the East End. This poor creature had probably starved to death in somebody's lock-up. Sadly, this was what happened to a lot of the animals when their racing days were over. So we gave it a new home, and it came to live with us in Myrdle Street. We had it hanging on the wall of our bedroom.

◇ In the context of Sir John Soane's Museum it immediately relates to three of the more curious items that Soane collected as noted in the Museum's 1837 Inventory: *'two [mummified] cats, one found in a house in Lothbury taken down for the new buildings at the Bank in 1803 between the wall and the wainscoting of a Room with the Rat in its mouth and the other in Lord Yarborough's House in Chelsea.'* It was relatively common to seal the body of a cat inside the wall of a building to ward off evil spirits. However, it is rather less common to extract them and install them in a small vitrine outside your bedroom as Soane did, and where they can still be seen today.

While a singular curiosity, the mummified cats do also relate to the strong narrative of trauma and death that runs through the Museum: from the sarcophagus and Sepulchral Chamber to the references to Mrs Soane, who died in 1815, twenty-two years before her husband, in almost every room.

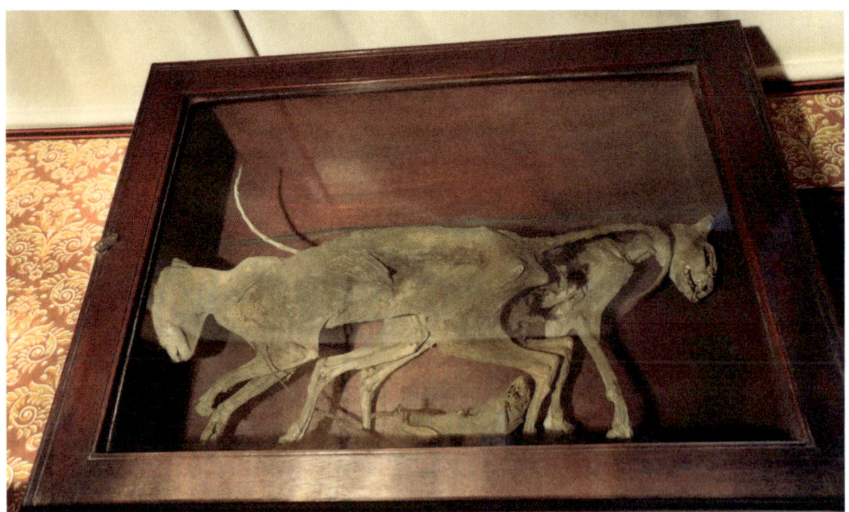

Two mummified cats and a rat posed in a glazed case, Sir John Soane's Museum, London, 2020

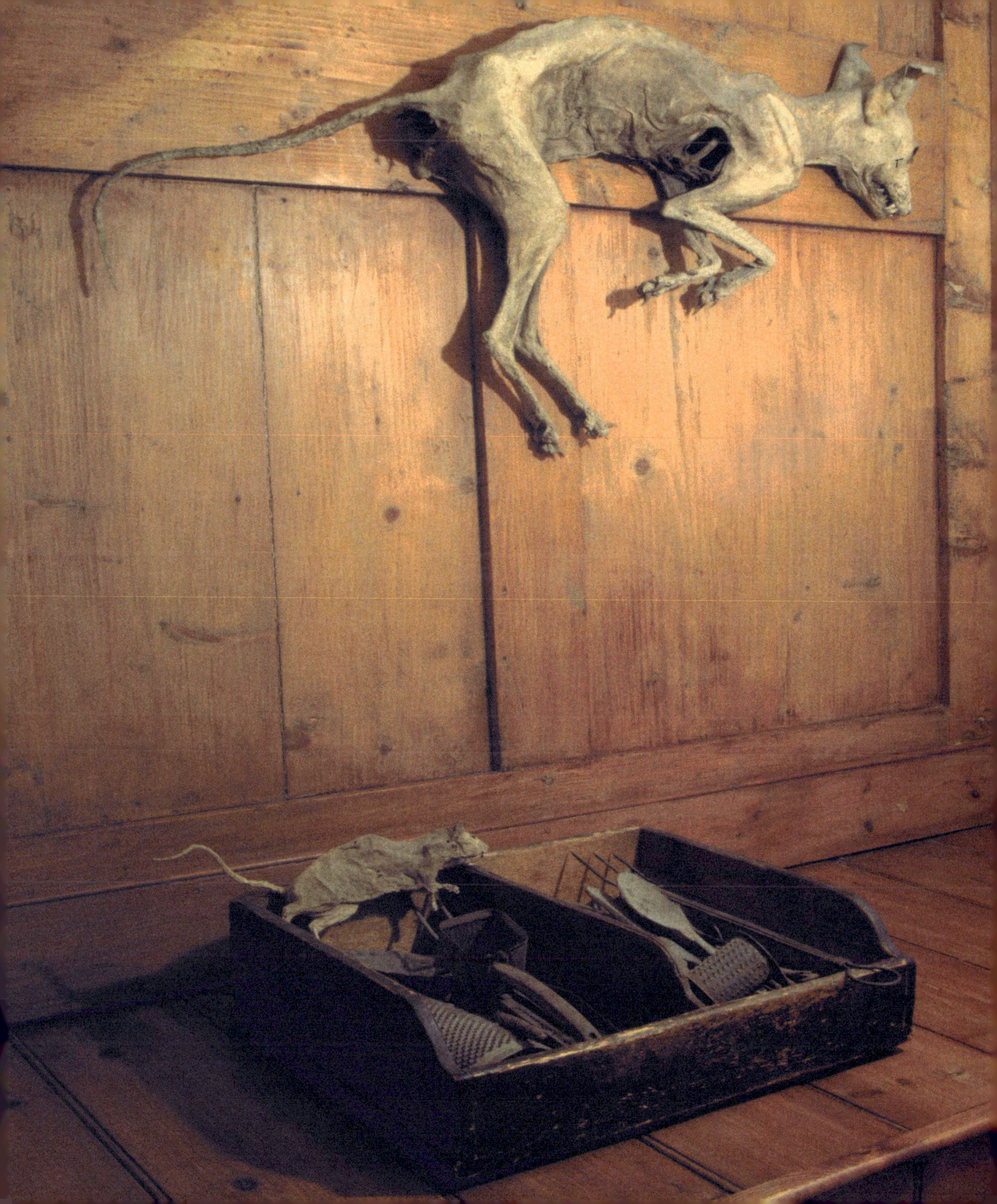

Many of the 'found objects' we've collected are, of course, also records of trauma. One work in particular – the *Burnt Madonna* – came to us as the result of an arson attack at a Roman Catholic church in Suffolk on Christmas Day in 1985. Nikki's mother attended the church and she saved it. Now it's one of our most treasured possessions.

We call her the *Burnt Madonna*, but she's actually Saint Theresa of the Roses, because she's still clutching a posy of roses despite the fact she's been burned. The charring of the wood is evidence of a kind of suffering. She personally means a lot to us because she was just inside the entrance to our house in Myrdle Street and now plays a similar role in a completely different modern setting at *Untitled* our studio in Kent.

Although the *Burnt Madonna* is a 'found object', burning is a tactic you've used purposefully in your work, for example *Burnt Interlocking Chairs* 1997.

There's definitely a connection, even if it's subliminal, between these works. We'd actually worked with burnt things before this. As part of our degree show at Hornsey College of Art in 1980 we showed a whole installation of burnt books in burnt bookcases taken from a bookshop in north London that had burned down. The installation was incredibly beautiful with the dark patinas of the charring. But unfortunately our art school burnt down too, so it all got burnt again and nothing survived that time.

Also burning is an interesting counterpoint to the pristine, white lacquer that we use for our furniture sculpture. The burnt versions become a kind of dark reflection.

They are also suggestive of absence while retaining a strong material presence. It's a feeling that's evoked by works like *Adjoining Rooms* 1989 where there is also a sense of potential.

Adjoining Rooms 1989 follows *Traces of Living* 1986, which is three tables with objects under glass like vitrines, but with *Adjoining Rooms* the three tables are left empty. We also incorporated panels of clear acrylic in the primary colours of red, yellow and blue in the sides so that the mechanism of display, rather than the objects displayed, becomes the focus. It could also be endless. You could adjoin so many colours. You could carry on infinitely.

We've made other sculptures with vitrines that are empty, such as *Conversation Seat* 1986 and *Negotiating Table* 1991. It's really about the potential of space and it reinforces the idea that the object itself is the subject for contemplation.

And the potential of the work. The viewer is left in a sense to fill the void, to infer an object or activity that's somehow latent within it.

Burnt Madonna at **Untitled**, Kent, 2019

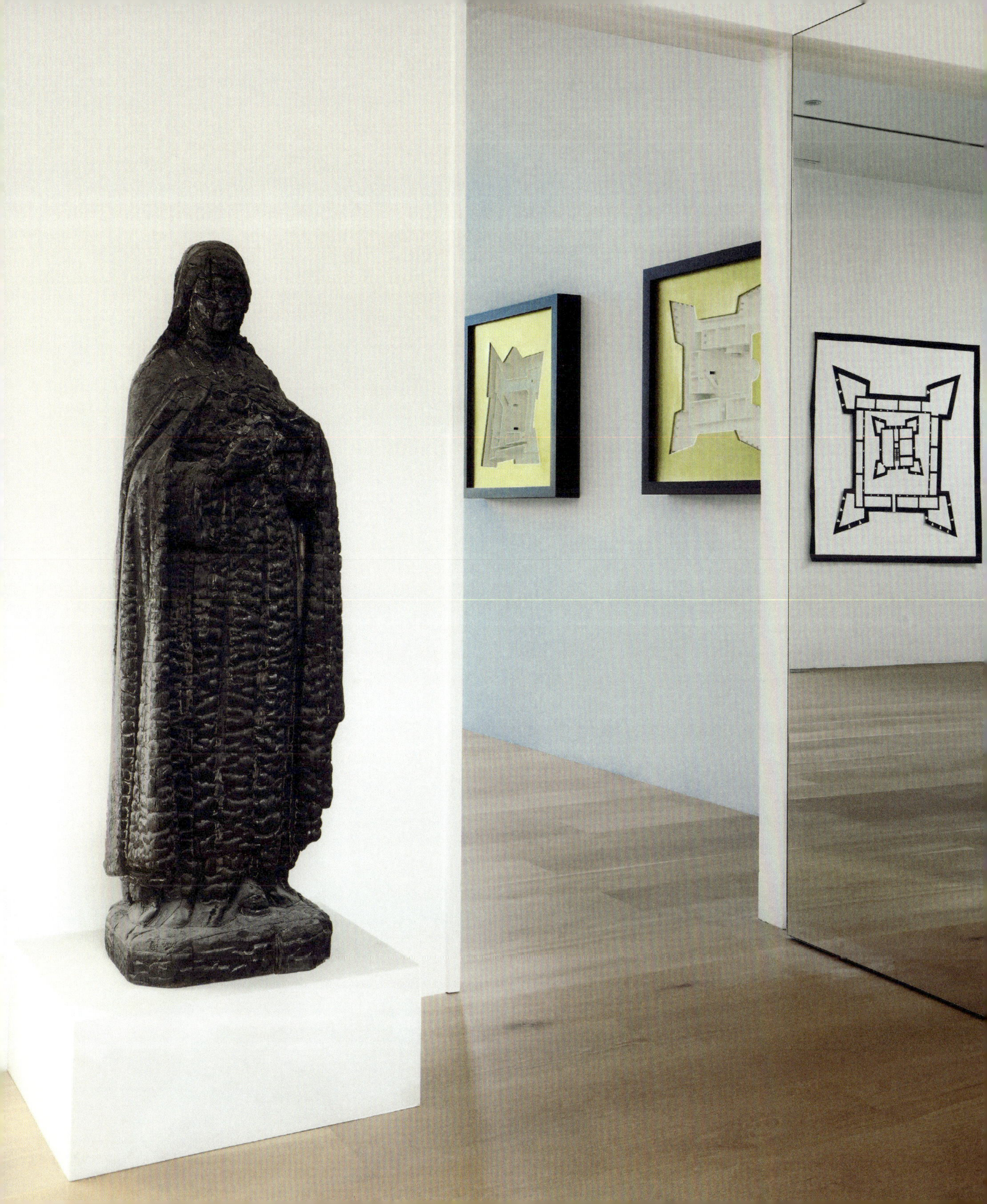

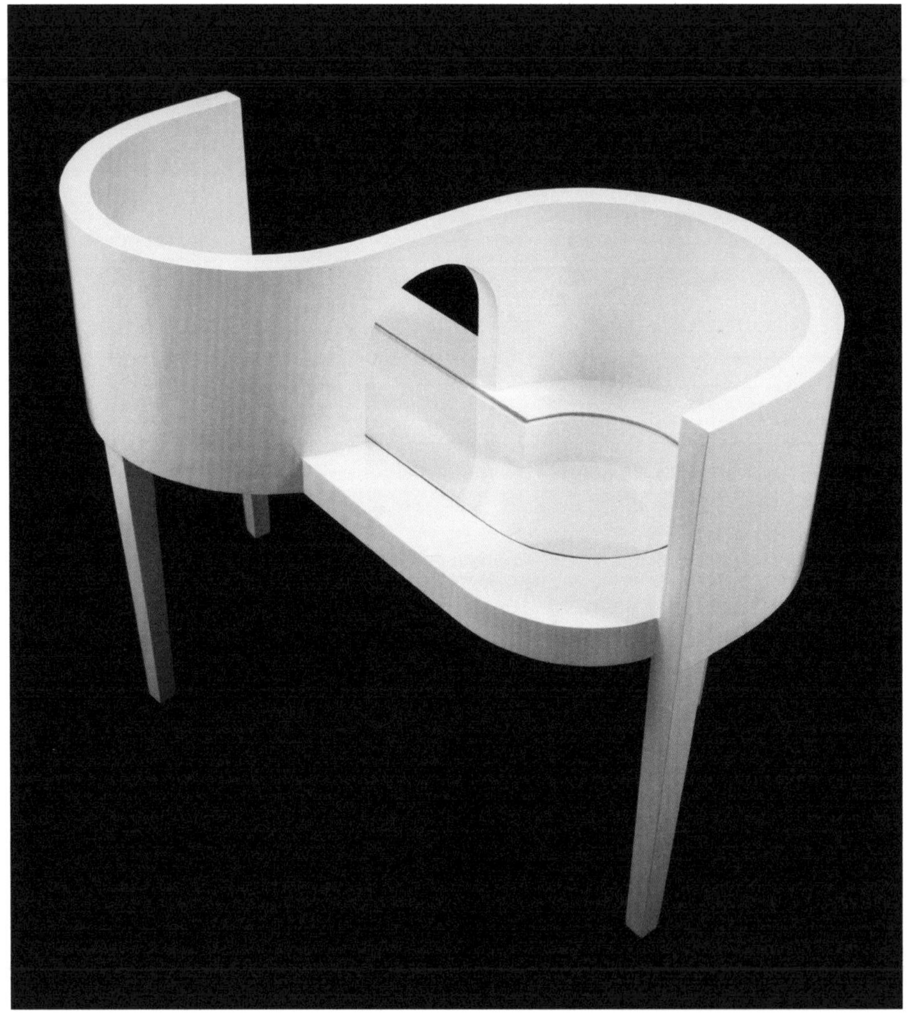

Conversation Seat 1986

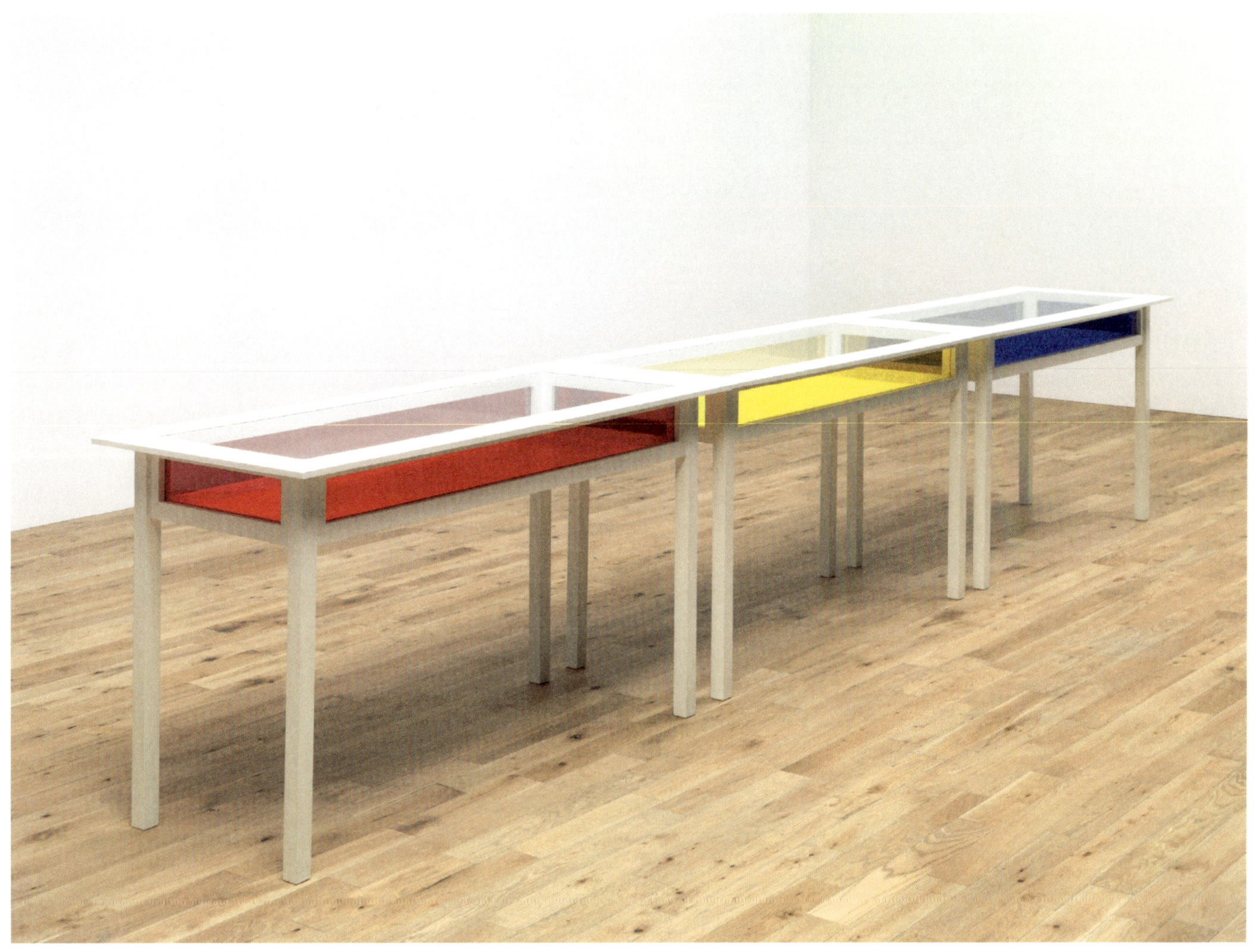

Adjoining Rooms 1989

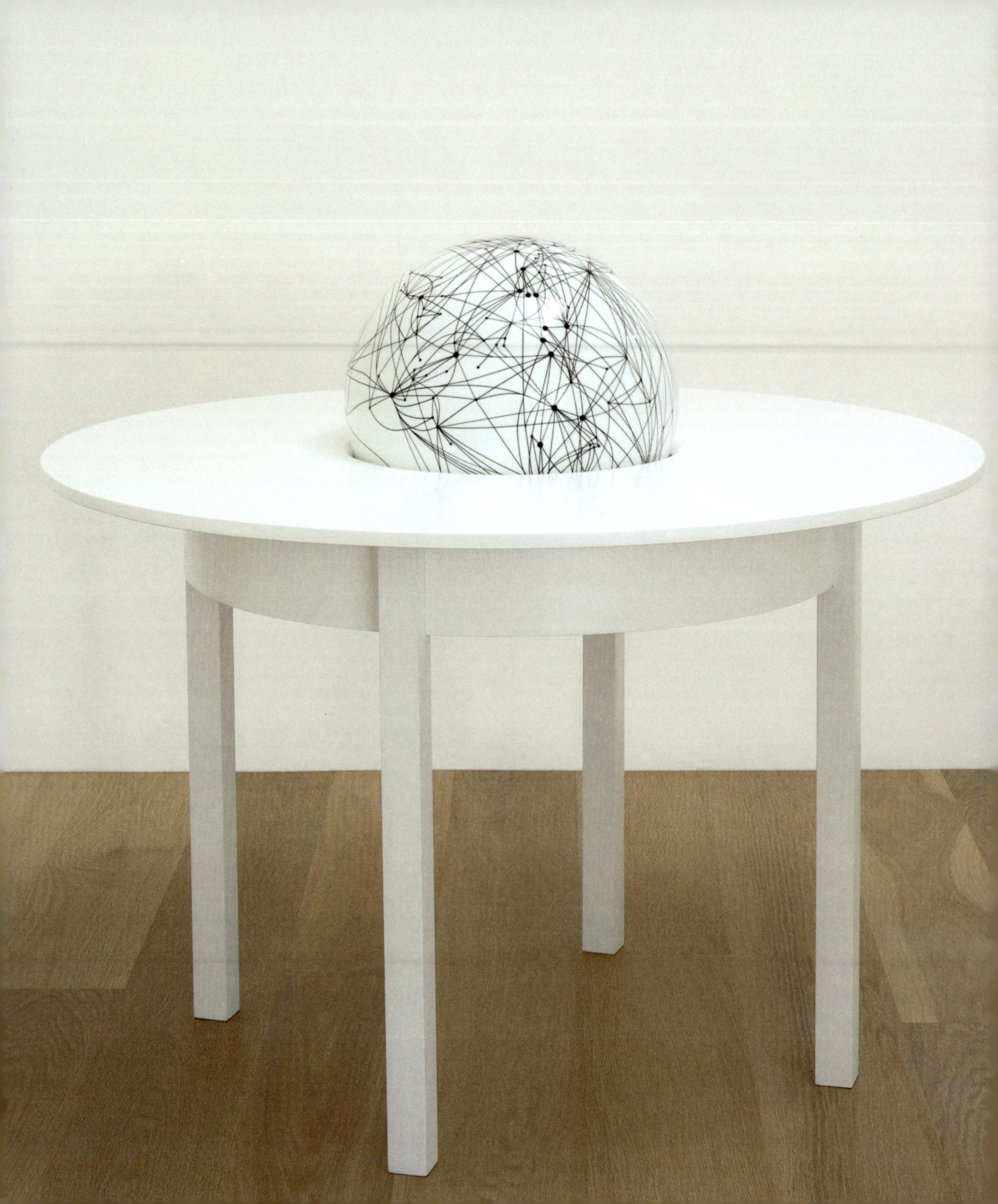

Revealing the invisible

◇ The notion of travel is at the very core of the Museum. It's both the means through which all these objects were brought together and it's also the sensation they are intended to evoke as visitors enter into the heterotopic space that constitutes the Museum. There's perhaps an inherent challenge in putting one's finger on something that is by its very nature transient. It's been a recurring interest of yours, which you've explored in the *Air Routes* series – which in a sense are maps formed by plotting the routes taken by commercial aeroplanes across the UK, Europe and the world.

○ The *Air Routes* are something we've worked with quite regularly since 1989. They're about international communication and exchange, the arrangement of routes of access and their visual projections. They are the architecture of the sky.

They are based in reality, but they also appear very abstract the first time you see them – there's little sense of the familiar political geography and physical geography. You're not sure what you're looking at, and then it begins to take shape.

The new work we've made for the No.13 Breakfast Room continues the series. It's a circular table with a globe that can be moved by one or two people in any direction. It's not rotating on one axis. It points everywhere at once.

◇ It powerfully conveys this is new global geography. It presents a world of hubs and connections between them in which are encoded economic, cultural and social relations. I'm interested in how you've applied this ongoing enquiry to a globe table, a quite familiar type of furniture which is redolent of historic settings.

○ Visitors are not normally supposed to touch the exhibits, but, in this case, they're being invited to do so. The Breakfast Room is the space around which the Museum turns, from there you can branch out and follow whichever route you like. We were very struck by the room's extraordinary domed ceiling. It was a new kind of dome that Soane developed. And, of course, domes, architecturally, are symbolic of the celestial sphere and the heavens and what's going on above us. There's a connection in that sense between the globe and the dome. The many mirrors in the room create this kind of strange surveillance.

◇ You appear in multiple mirrors at once. It's like the way we exist in the online world: the fragmentation of ourselves into an infinitude of reflections. I'm interested in the way the presence of your work in this historic interior – and the dialogue established between the two – unlocks a whole series of interpretations of the space that would be hard to sustain without it.

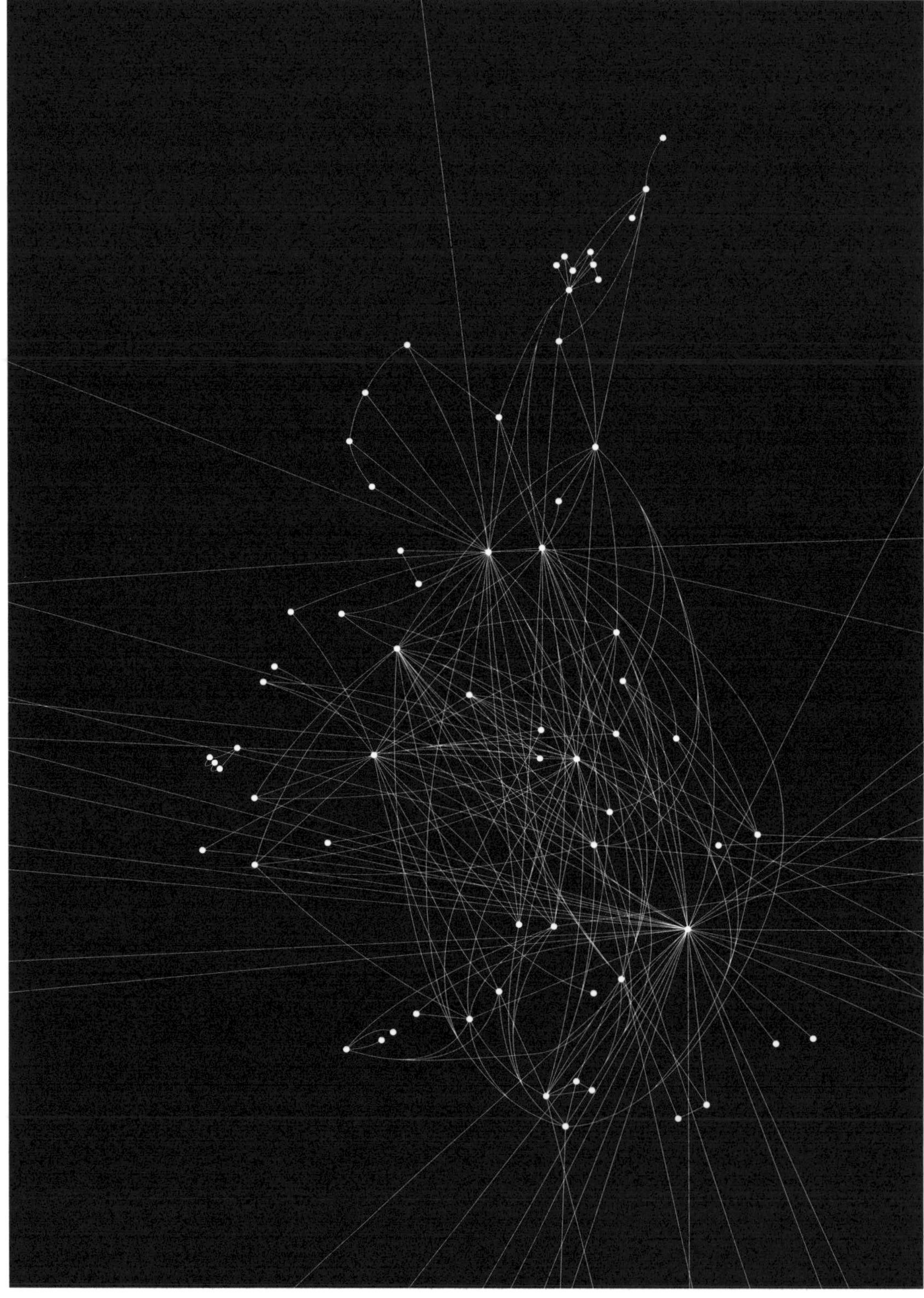

Air Routes of Britain (Night) 2000

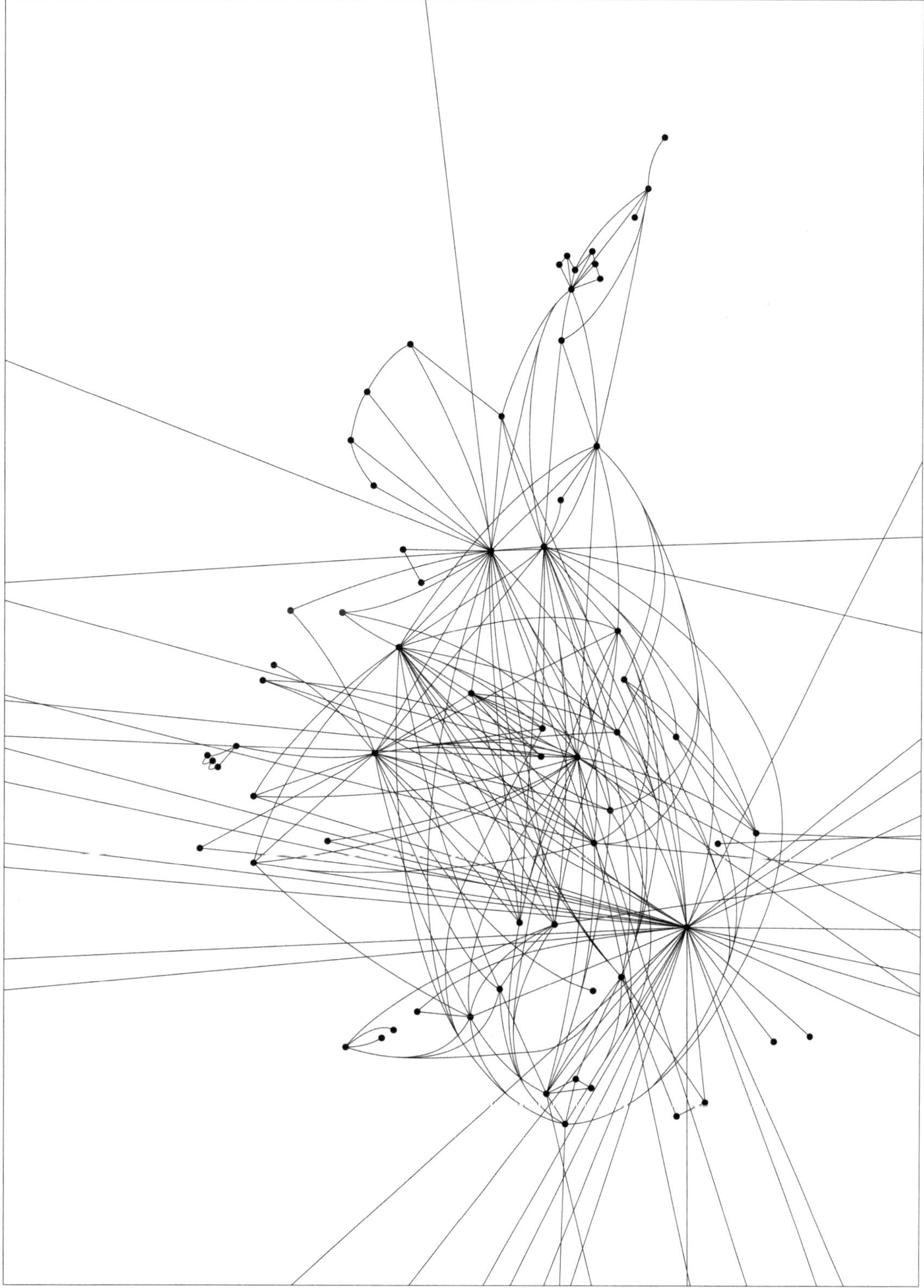

Air Routes of Britain (Day) 2000

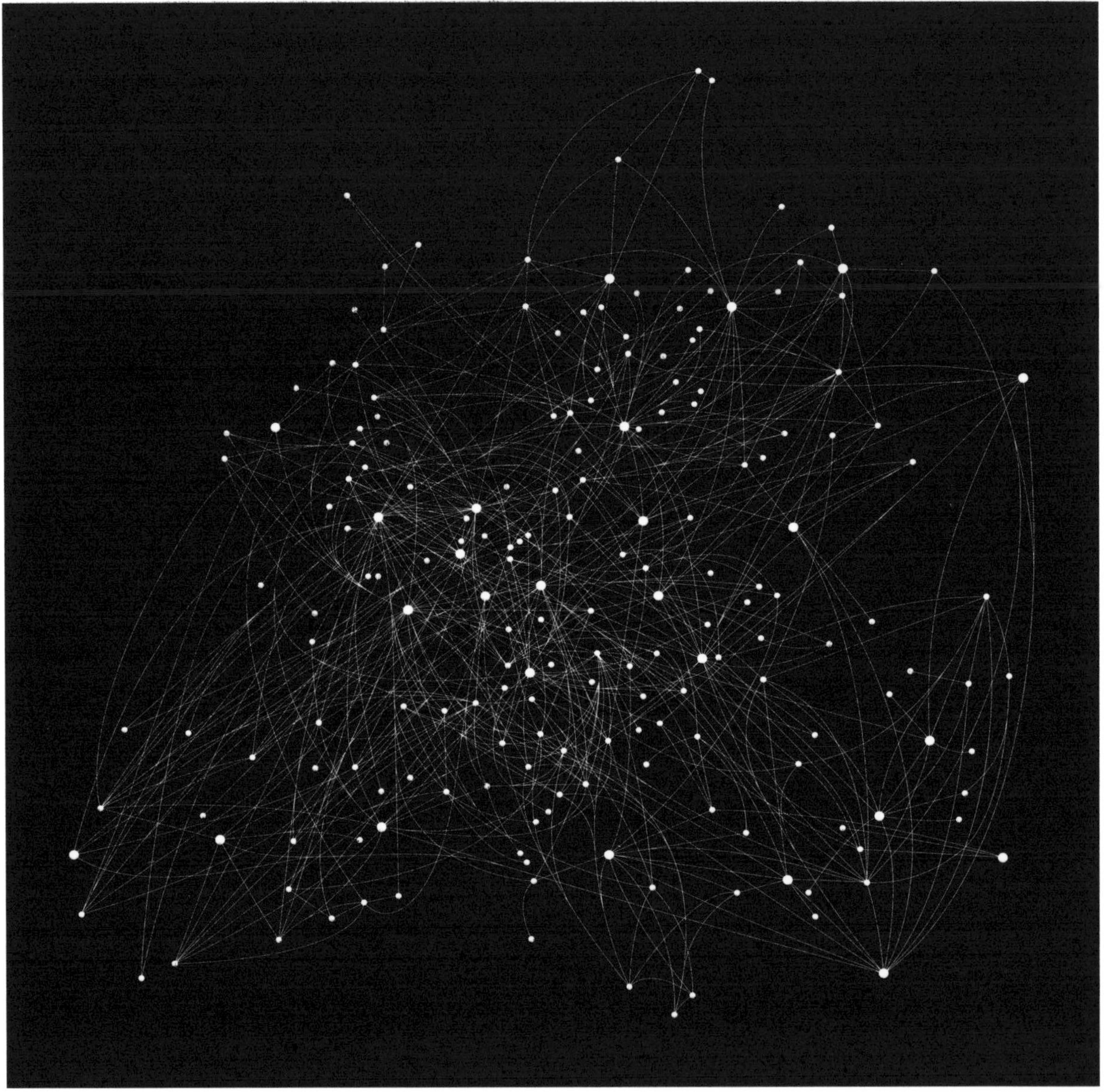

Air Routes of Europe (Night) 2002–20

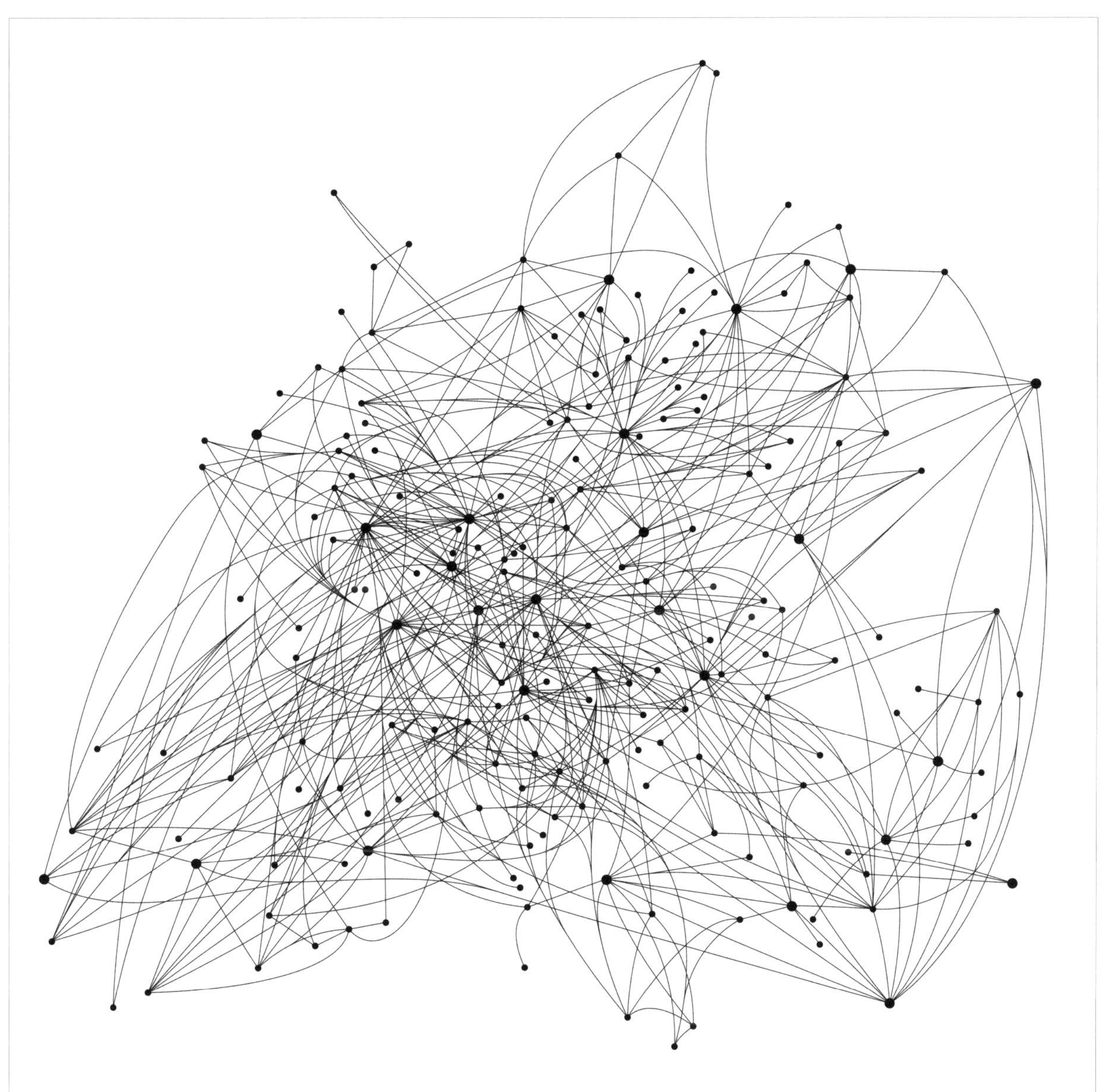

Air Routes of Europe (Day) 2002–20

We are also displaying *Virtual World* 2009, a medal commissioned by the British Museum for the *Medals of Dishonour* exhibition in 2009. When we received the commission, we visited their extraordinary medal collection and saw medals in a new way.

One typically thinks of medals as something awarded for special acts of valour or achievement, yet from the Renaissance onwards they were commissioned by the European power-elite as a kind of portable portraiture, or selfie even. They fulfilled some of the roles that photos do today for communicating, memorialising and propagandising certain individuals, causes or events. However, because the people who could afford to have medals made were wealthy and powerful popes, dukes and princes, etc. they are a portrait of the historical status quo – the established power. Precisely because of this, medals were also made in opposition by renegade and subversive tendencies, anti-Hanoverian Jacobites, those opposed to Napoleon, or anti-World War I agitators in Germany.

That led us to the idea of making a medal that was a reflection on today's geo-strategic power relationships, and the way they're so ubiquitous and so disembodied in the globalised contemporary world. We're all connected by multiple grids and systems of information and administration. And as the world gets more complicated, we have more and more need to simplify and codify, to abbreviate elements and events.

These codes and acronyms become avatars for the real world – with their own set of associations and connotations.

The medal is titled *Virtual World* and combines three categories of codes; codes for airports around the world, like LHR or JFK or LAX. Then there are the codes of NGOs involved in reconstruction and disaster relief like UN, WHO or USAID. And, finally, there are the codes of banned organisations and security agencies, IRA, CIA, ETA, ISIS, etc. On the obverse are the country codes for top-level internet domains, .uk, .it, .fr, etc. The work brings these all into relation and posits them as a new language of the structures that are increasingly ordering our lives.

There's something very powerful about how this largely intangible, immaterial world of networks, connections and systems is then crystallised in this very particular kind of object with this very particular history. This duality is further explored by where the work is displayed in the Breakfast Room.

There's this peculiar shrine to Napoleon on the south wall. Soane was clearly taken with Napoleon as a kind of Romantic hero, the corporal who through his personal charisma and abilities, rose to an incredibly powerful position, before ending in exile and failure. There's this personal story, which Soane clearly

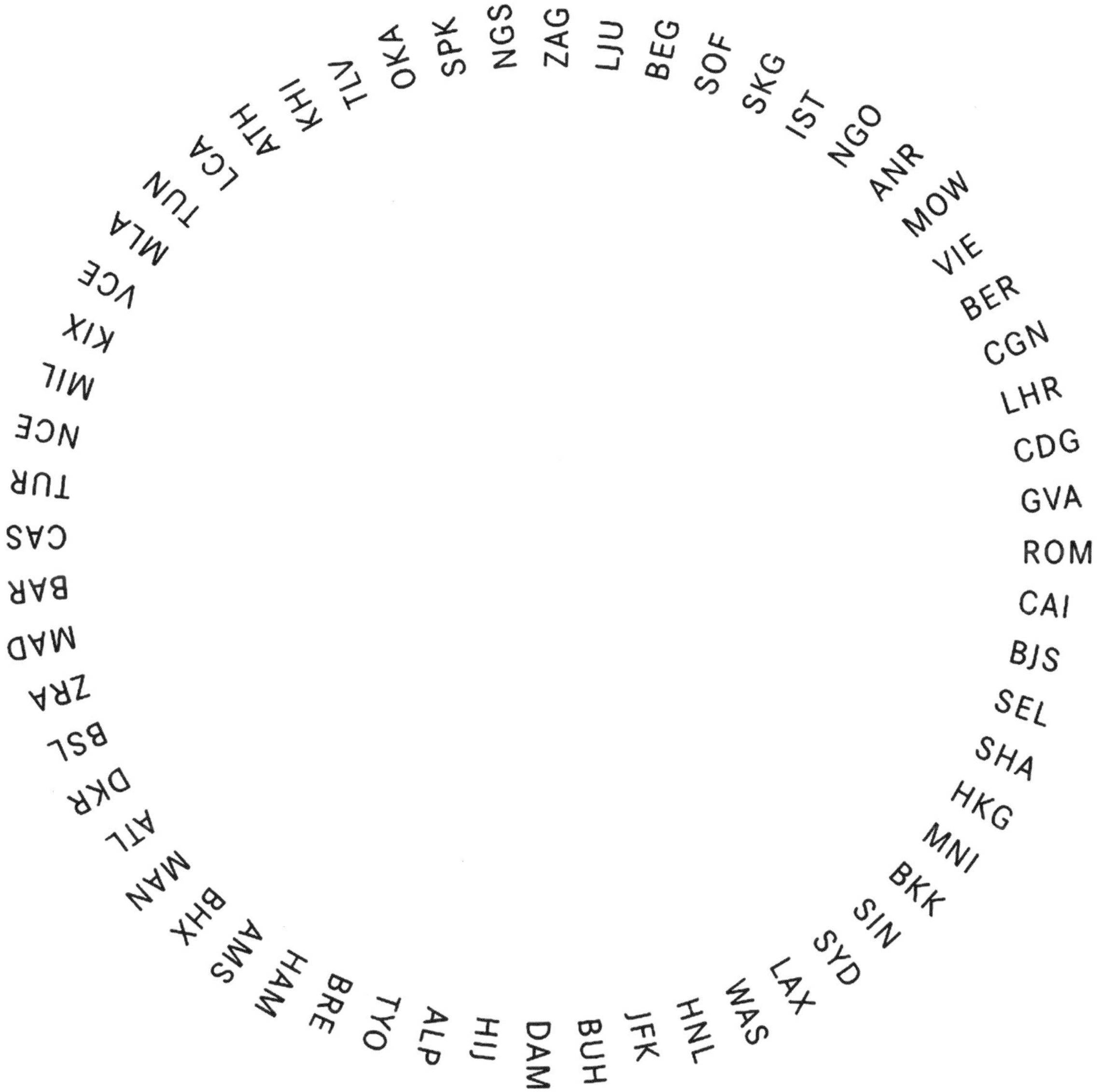

LJU BEG SOF SKG IST NGO ANR MOW VIE BER CGN LHR CDG GVA ROM CAI BJS SEL SHA HKG MNI BKK SIN SYD LAX WAS HNL JFK BUH DAM HIJ ALP TYO BRE HAM AMS BHX MAN ATL DKR BSL ZRA MAD BAR CAS TUR NCE MIL KIX VCE MLA TUN LCA ATH KHI TLV OKA SPK NGS ZAG

Frozen Sky (Day) 2000

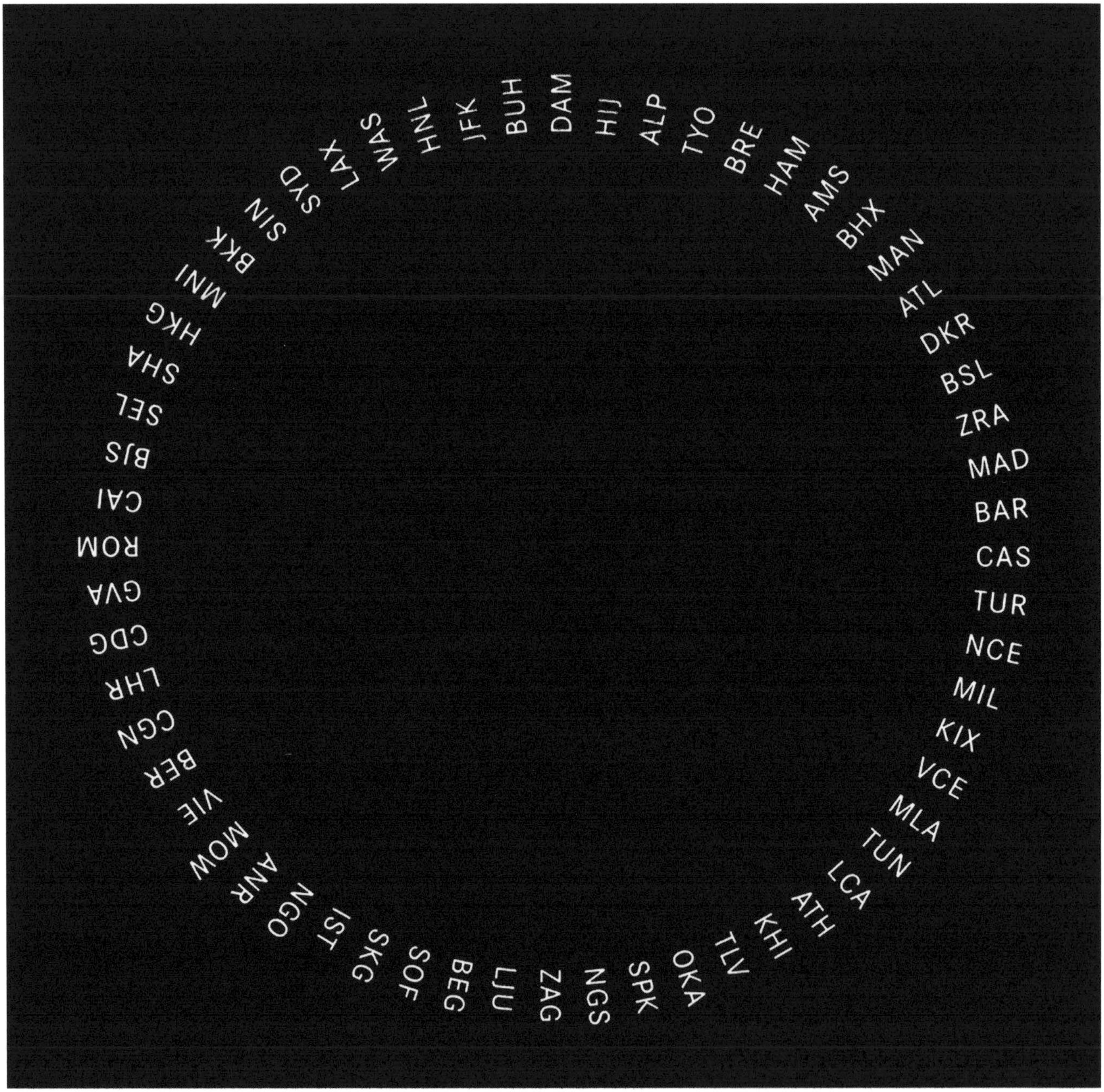

BUH DAM HIJ ALP TYO BRE HAM AMS BHX MAN ATL DKR BSL ZRA MAD BAR CAS TUR NCE MIL KIX VCE MLA TUN LCA ATH KHI TLV OKA SPK NGS ZAG LJU BEG SOF SKG IST NGO ANR MOW VIE BER CGN LHR CDG GVA ROM CAI BJS SEL SHA HKG MNI BKK SIN SYD LAX WAS HNL JFK

Frozen Sky (Night) 2000

identified with, but one that also speaks to the political relationships and geostrategic power relationships in Europe and the world at that time in history.

We're displaying the medals in the box that sits at the centre of the composition, which originally contained a pistol that, as the inscription records, was 'taken by Peter the Great, Emperor of all the Russians, from Bey, Commander of the Turkish Army at Azof, 1696 And presented by Alexander Emperor of Russia to Napoleon Bonaparte, Emperor of France, at the Treaty of Tilsit, 1807. And presented to a Gentleman by Napoleon at St Helena, 1820'. The case is empty because the pistol was stolen in 1969.

◇ There are remarkable symmetries here: the pistol a kind of 'found object', of interest to Soane because of its history, the fact it was held by Napoleon, as opposed to its significance as a pistol; and an empty vitrine with the potential to be filled and new meanings created or revealed. The empty vitrine is a void – literally and metaphorically – to fill.

○ The fact the box remains empty – it has never been filled since the pistol was taken – allows us to add something that relates to the history that surrounds us and to the world outside.

◇ Part of which, of course, is the perennial question of Britain's relationship to Europe and the rest of the world, a question with a long and constantly evolving history.

○ We've made many works that look at the architecture of international political institutions. At the outset we were looking in particular at the architecture of pan-European institutions and international organisations. It was the moment when the EEC (European Economic Community) was mutating into the European Union. We were interested in capturing this moment of evolution from economic to supra-national political entity. We began to explore how the architecture of these institutions reflected this change and we made sculptures of some of the buildings: *European Parliament* 1989, *Eurotempo* 1990, *European Court of Human Rights* 1991 and *International Court of Justice* 1991. One of them is in this exhibition: *The Council of Europe* which we made 1989. It is a foreshortened perspective view of the hemicycle debating chamber.

◇ It takes on a metaphorical quality in the work: a circle where the two ends never meet; politics as a project that's never resolved.

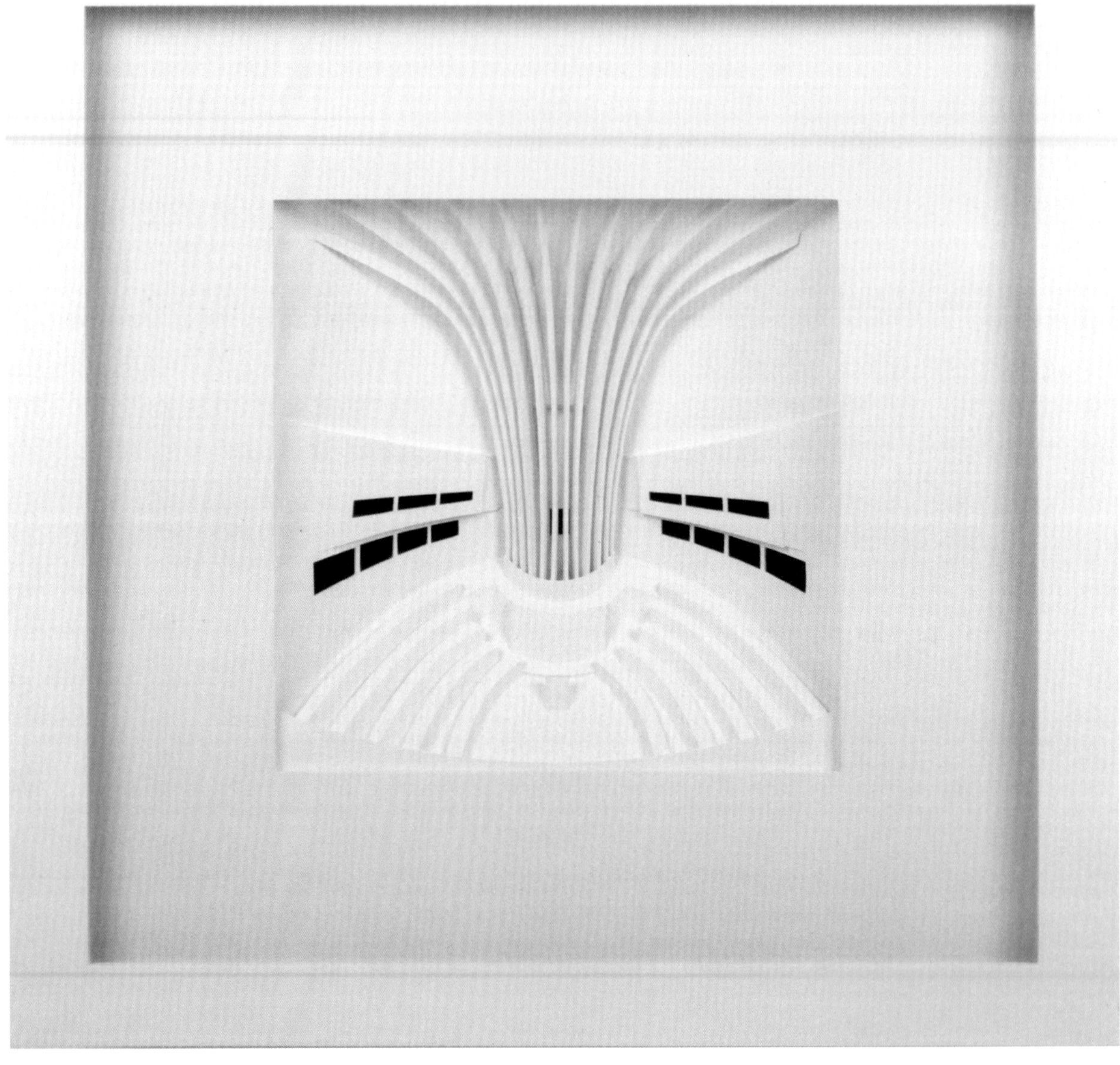

Council of Europe 1989

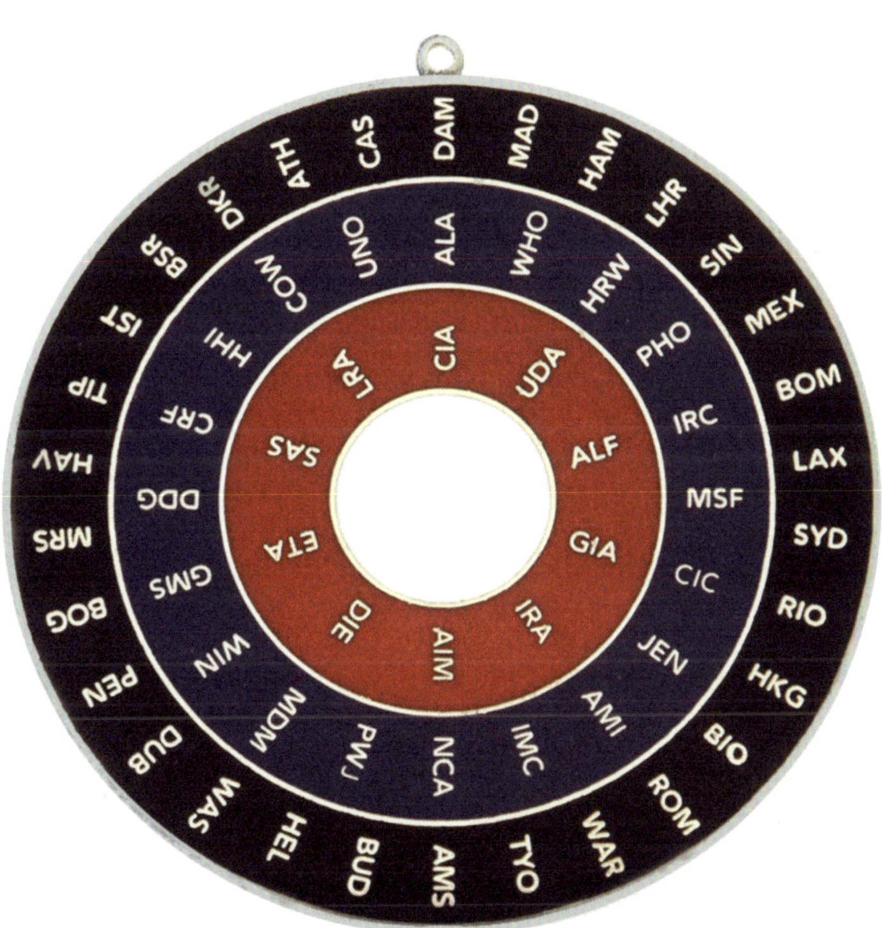

Virtual World, Medal of Dishonour 2008

Following pages
Virtual World, Medal of Dishonour in the Breakfast Room at Sir John Soane's Museum, London, 2019

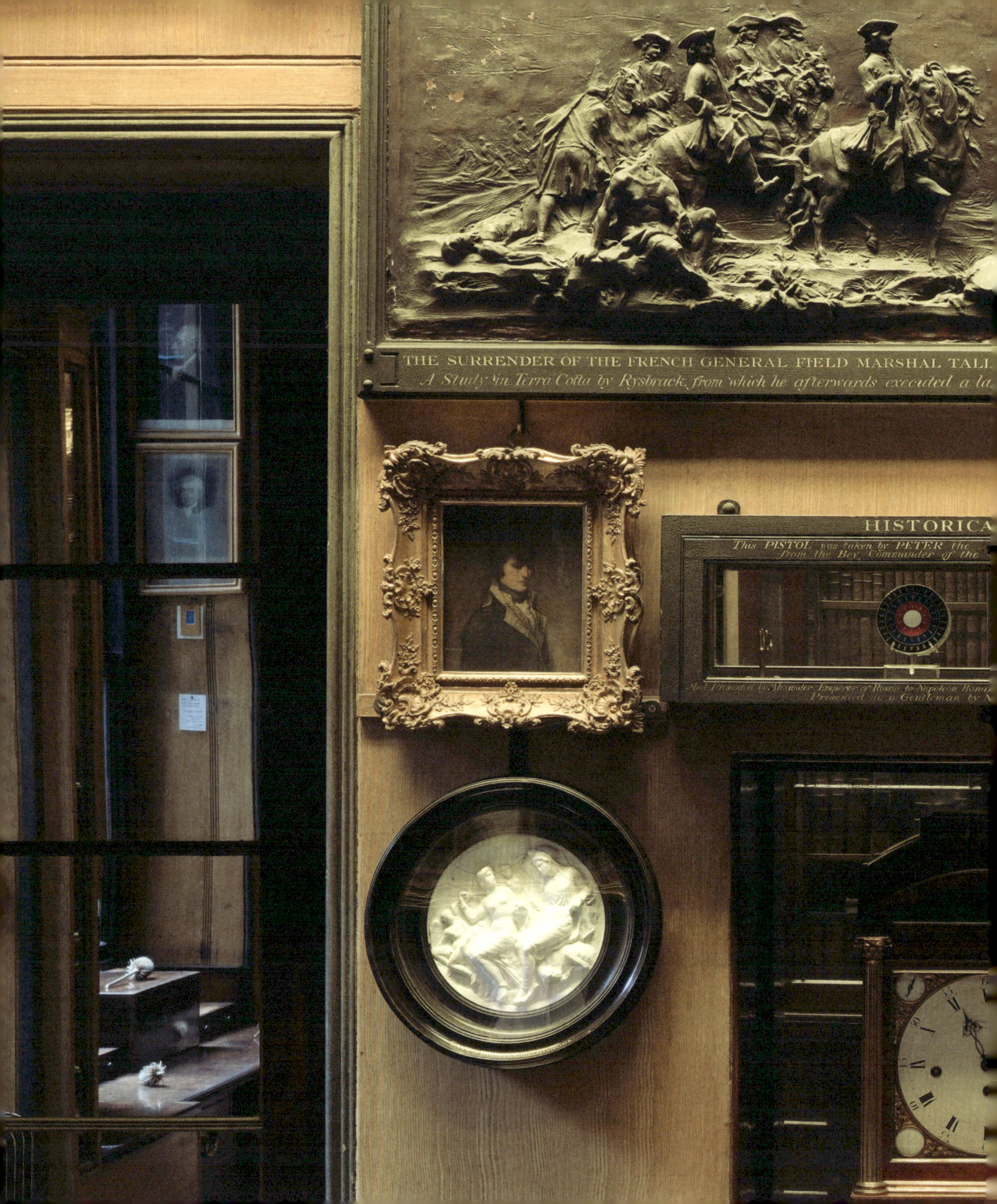
THE SURRENDER OF THE FRENCH GENERAL FIELD MARSHAL
A Study in Terra Cotta by Rysbrack, from which he afterwards executed a
HISTORICA
This PISTOL was taken by PETER the
from the Bey, Commander of the
And Presented by Alexander Emperor of Russia to Napoleon
Presented to a Gentleman by

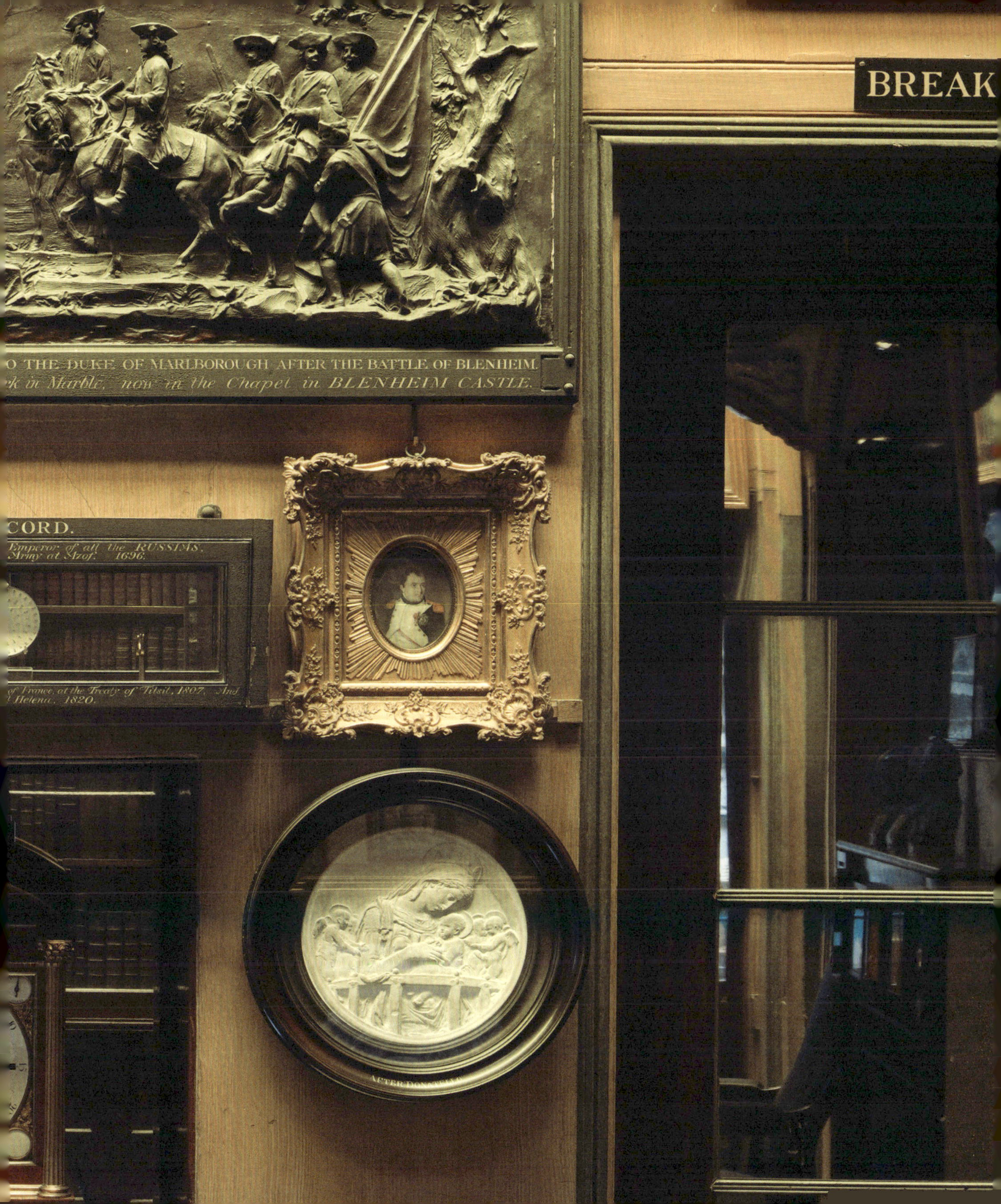
BREAK
O THE DUKE OF MARLBOROUGH AFTER THE BATTLE OF BLENHEIM.
k in Marble, now in the Chapel in BLENHEIM CASTLE.
CORD.
Emperor of all the RUSSIAS.
Army at Azof. 1696.
of France, at the Treaty of Tilsit, 1807. And
Helena. 1820.

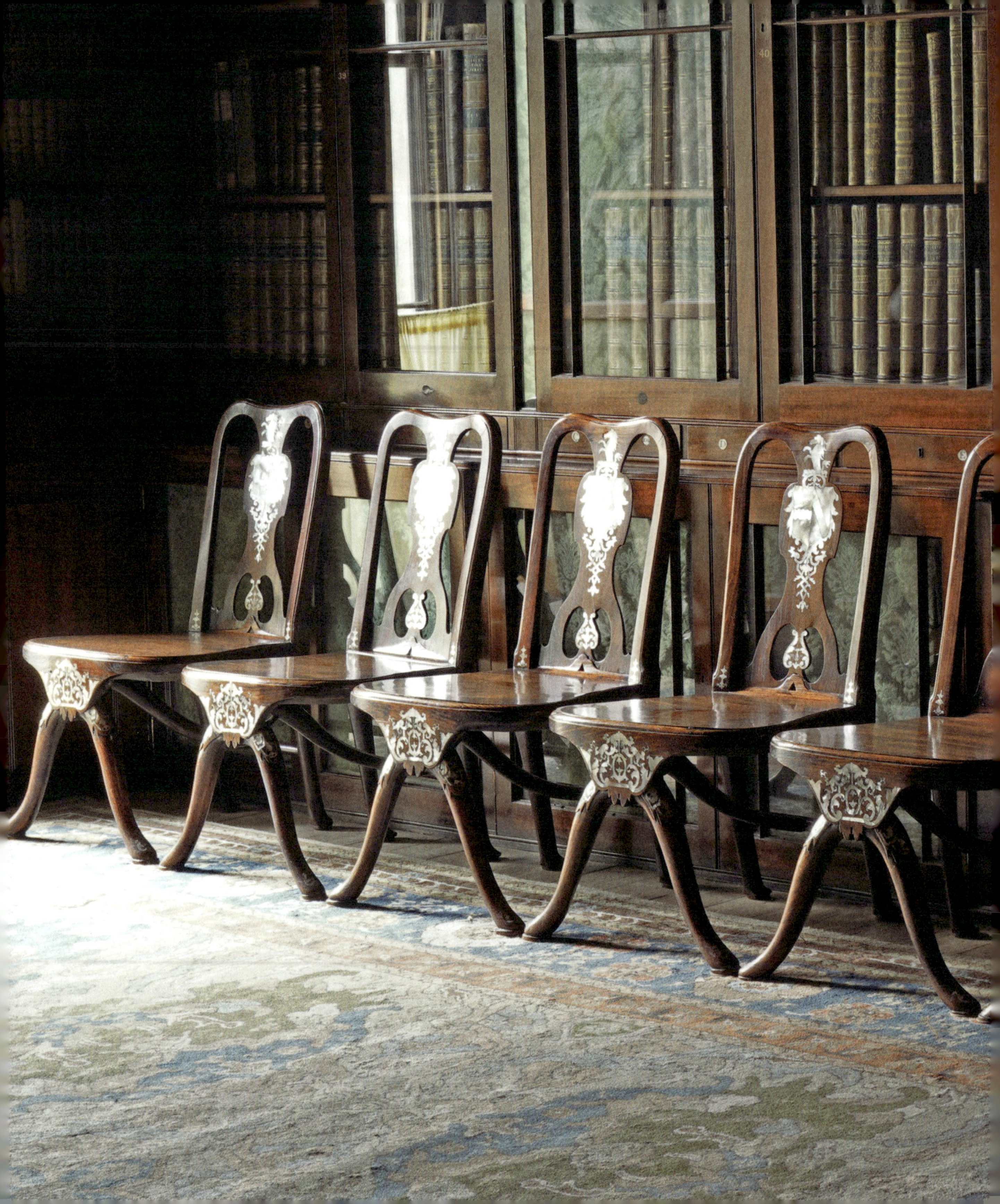
39
40

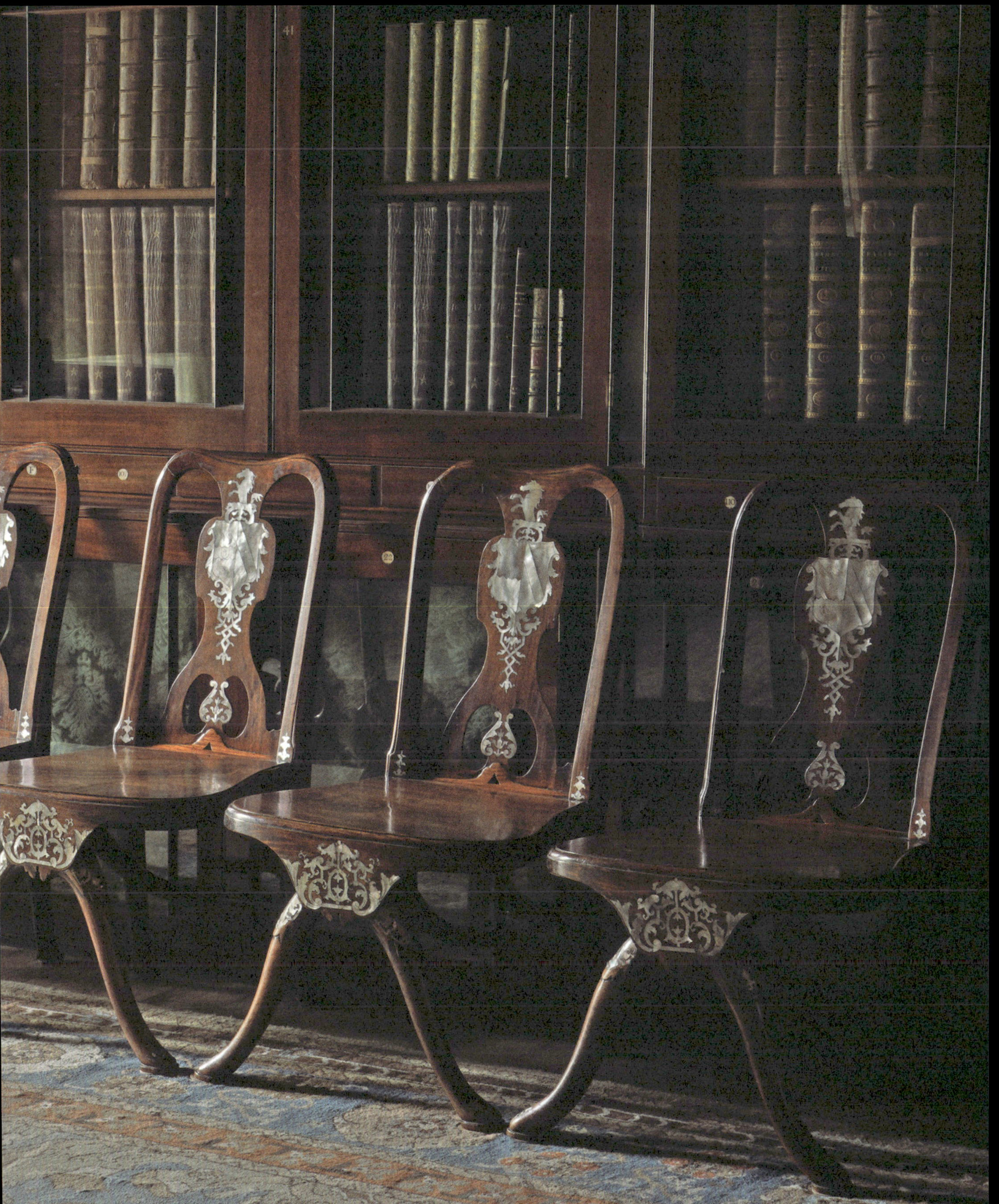

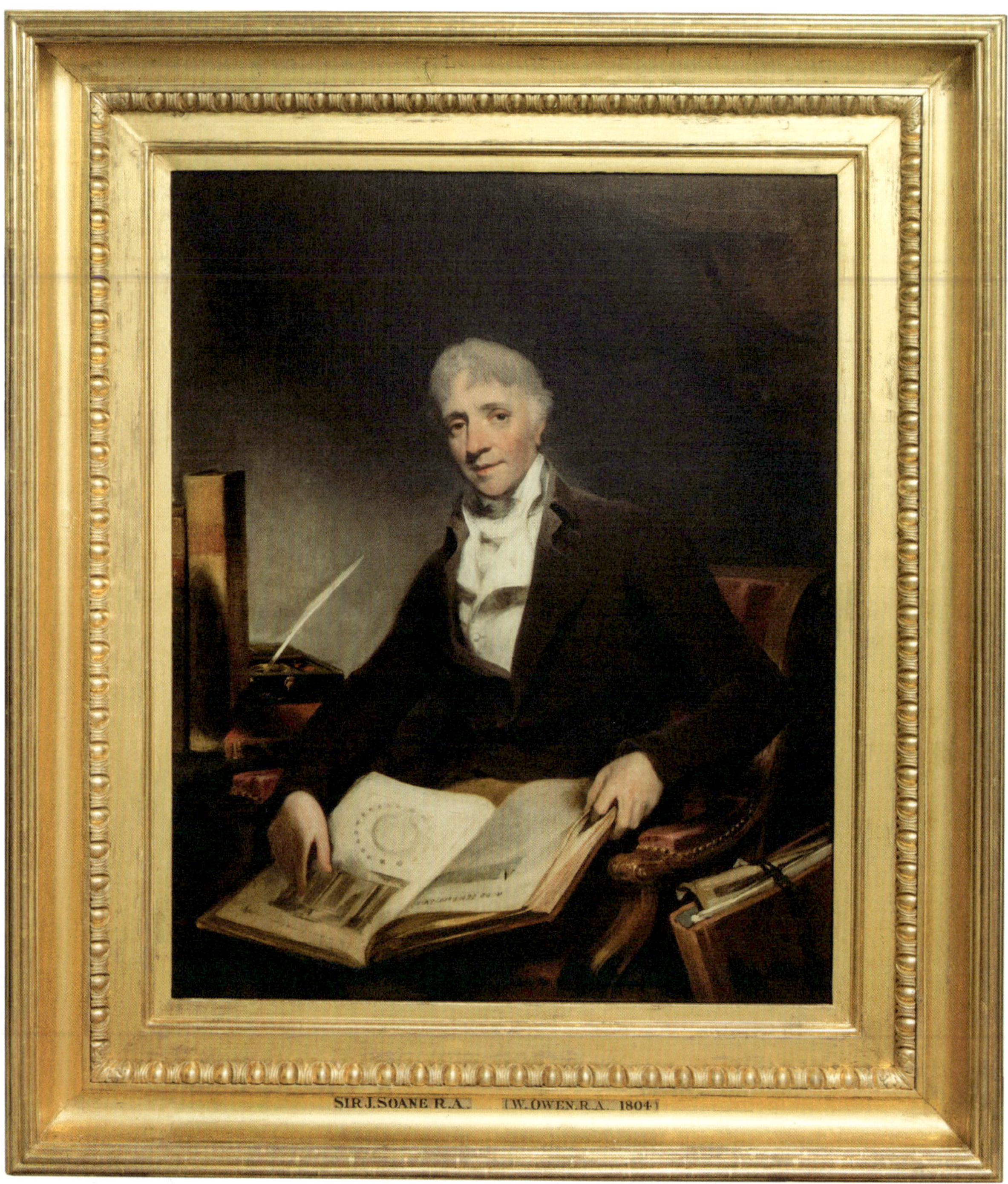

Portrait of Sir John Soane, William Owen, 1804

Previous pages
Soane's Cantonese chairs (c.1725–35) in the Library-Dining Room at Sir John Soane's Museum, London, 2019

Collapsing time

◇ For the most part there is a clear distinction in the Museum between furniture and works of art – at least in the overtly domestic spaces. An exception to this is the row of eight early eighteenth-century Cantonese chairs that are lined up against the west wall in the Library – rather more for display than for use as places to sit.

○ The first time we saw them, we were immediately struck by them and perhaps subliminally they influenced us in making two works – *Passed in the Present* 1987 and *Maisons de Force* 1990 – where we similarly worked with a row of chairs, seven in each case. Originally we assumed they were Soane's dining chairs and didn't realise that in this setting they were actually un-functional, that he was appreciating them simply as objects, that they spoke to him on an artistic level.

For this exhibition we wondered whether we might create a group of chairs that would temporarily replace Soane's. We were very interested in the itinerary of Soane's Grand Tour and the places he'd visited on his journey to and from and around Italy over 1778–80. There were the obvious places like the Temple of Vesta at Tivoli and the Villa Farnese at Caprarola, which we'd visited. We've also been architectural tourists, especially early in our career. Like Soane, we'd been to Milan, Zurich, Brussels, Cologne; in fact, some of our first shows were in these places so there was an interesting connection.

The next step was to find out what was happening in those places today, what was being built now. In some cases, we knew already: we'd been to Zurich and seen David Chipperfield's extension to the Kunsthaus under construction. We'd also seen and were quite struck by the Generali Tower in Milan by Zaha Hadid Architects. So, by bringing together a range of buildings – through their plans inserted into the seat of the chairs – we were able to link the classical past with the Renaissance, the Enlightenment and today.

◇ This linking of time periods is one of the Museum's most powerful aspects, bringing objects from very different periods and places into direct relation. It works a little like a city where buildings from totally different periods, different styles, different materials and different scales exist side-by-side in a kind of simultaneity.

○ A city like London. The Museum is very like London in that regard. It has that sensibility of being free to make these juxtapositions. In a lot of places – Paris for instance – it wouldn't feel legitimate or even possible to do these things aesthetically. The Museum has this radical discontinuity that we read as continuous.

◇ The tight relationship between the Museum and the city in which it is situated is certainly one of the reasons why it is of such interest to tourists and visitors to London.

○ We were visited about six months ago by an artist and curator from Switzerland who we had met when we were in Zurich. They'd been at a conference in Liverpool at Tate and they came to visit our studio on their way back to Heathrow. They said they were only in London for the rest of today and asked, 'what shall we do?' 'Go the Soane Museum', we responded. We had told them we were doing an exhibition there, but we knew they'd find it interesting anyway.

A couple of days later, we got an email from them. 'The place is amazing', they said, 'but what the hell will you do in that coral reef?!' That was how they saw it, as a kind of encrustation.

A lot of people do refer to the intensity of the Museum when they come here, and as artists it is a question of how to find space literally and metaphorically to show work. But the restrictions can sometimes give you freedom, forcing you to find a path through. This building is all about different routes, different options, and different ways to explore – we are simply adding some more.

◇ The occasional moments of rupture are incredibly important – they change how you see the work and how you see the setting. This takes on another dimension in the Museum, as opposed to the city, because it is entirely the work of one person; it is Soane's autobiography made spatial. It's something incredibly personal and individual that we're intervening in. But at the same time, every artist's work is autobiographical in some way.

○ We made the *Conversation Seat* at the end of 1985 and showed it first at Maureen Paley's gallery Interim Art in 1986. It was a very natural and intuitive attempt to make a sculpture that was in a way about us but also about architecture. Although it doesn't contain a model, it foreshadows our later work because it's almost a model in itself. It resembles a kind of modern pavilion. The glass surface set into the seat creates an empty vitrine which looks almost like a pool of water within a piece of 1930s modernist architecture, creating a fluid connection between the two halves.

Later, in 1989 and 1995 we made four different versions of *Interlocking Chairs*. There's a kind of mirroring in them which is quite like the first work we made together, *The Kitchen* 1978. It's a balancing of two equal parts. Some people have said they're a bit like an idealised self-portrait; at the very least there's an image of a relationship that's intertwined and in balance. The *Interlocking Chairs* became a kind of a signifier for our work together – very idealised and pared down.

Grand Tour (detail Bourse de Commerce) 2020

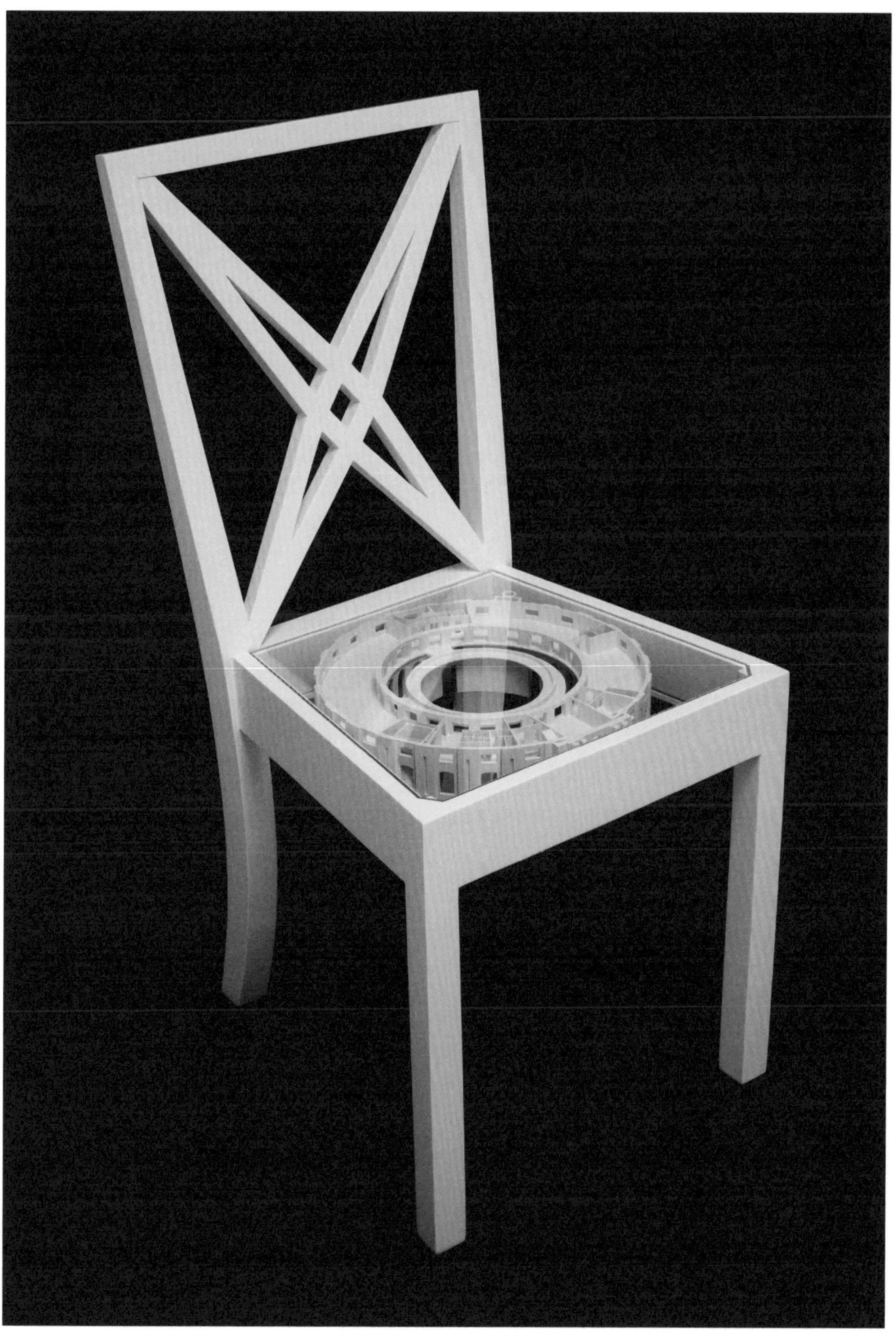

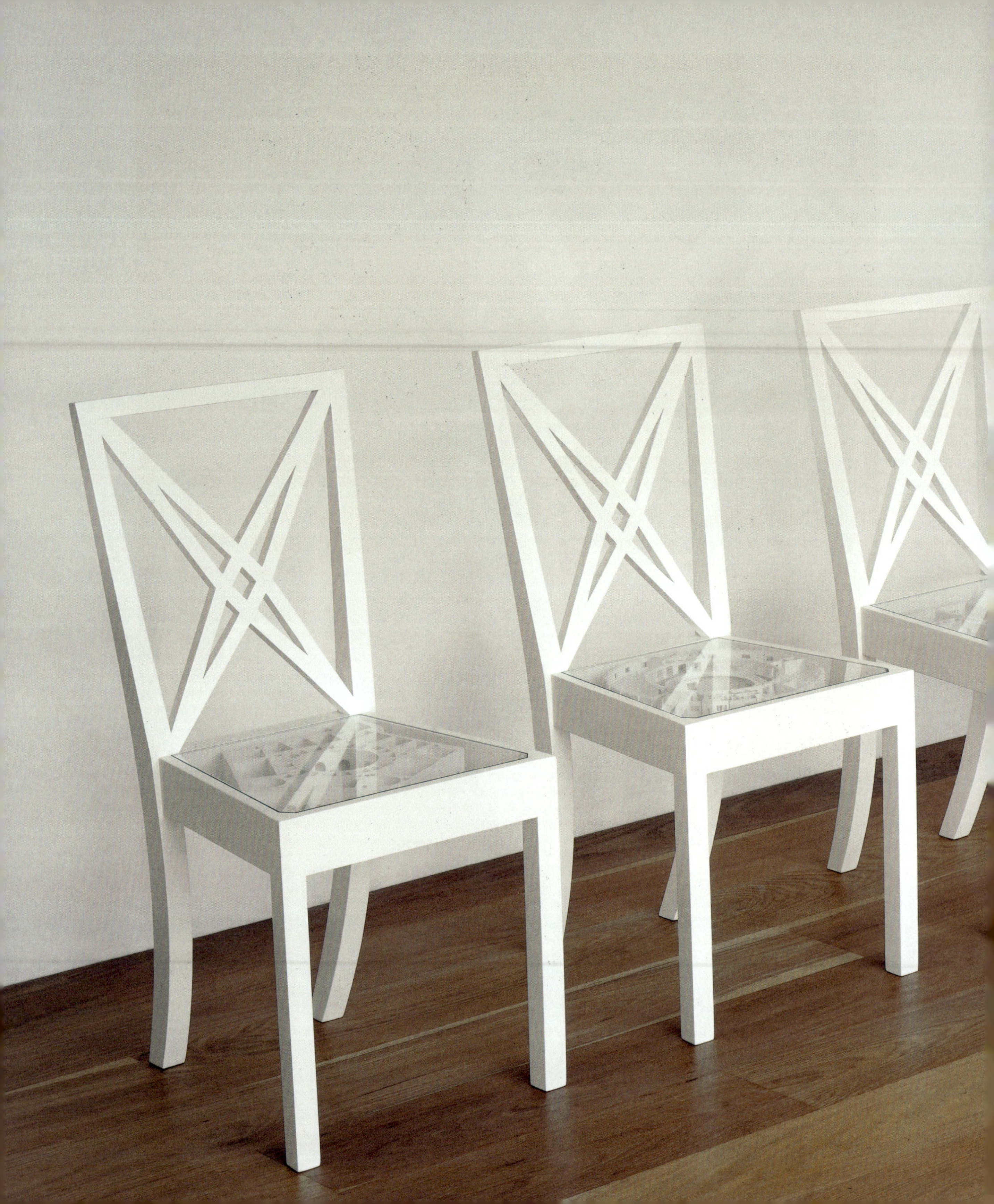

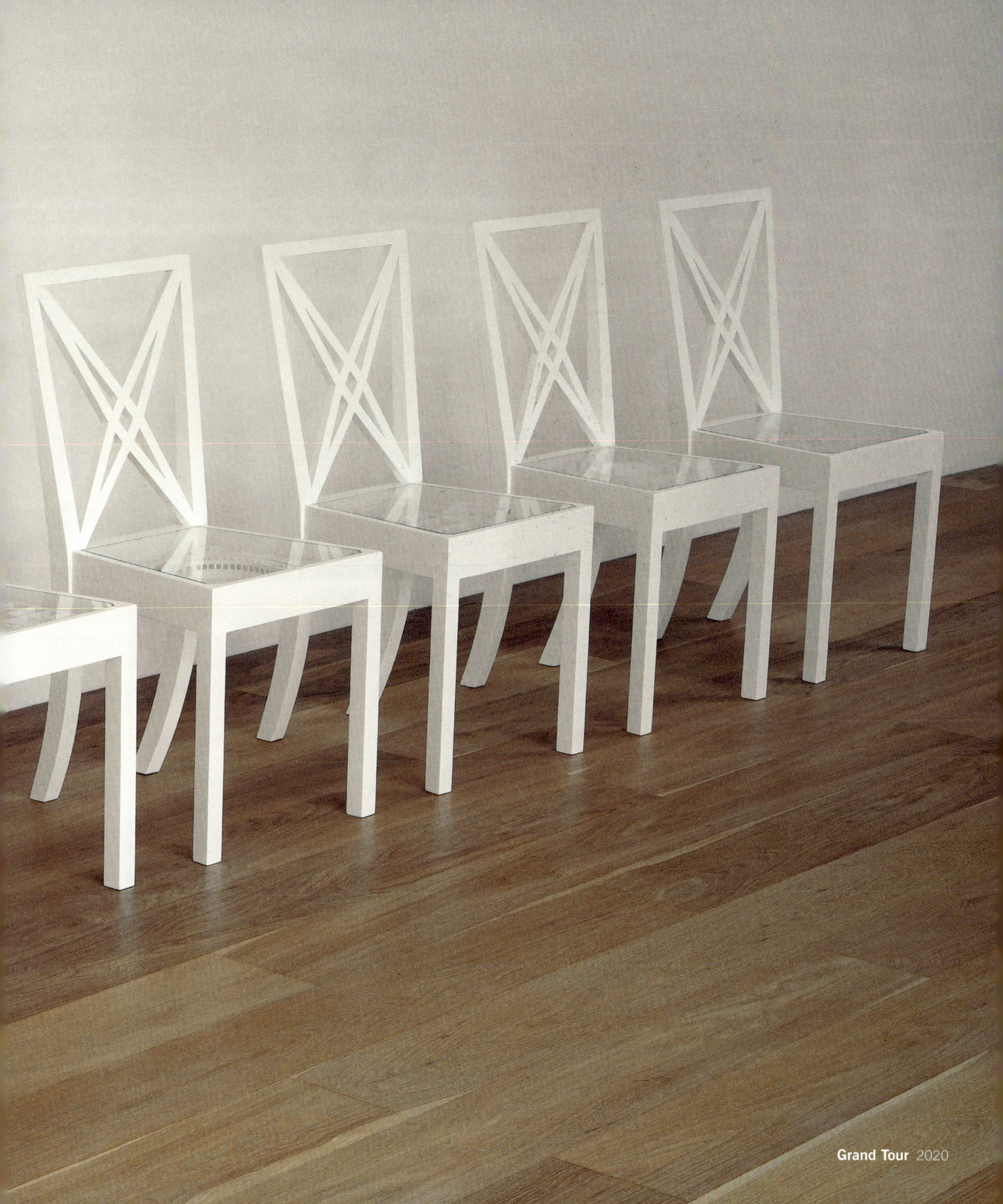

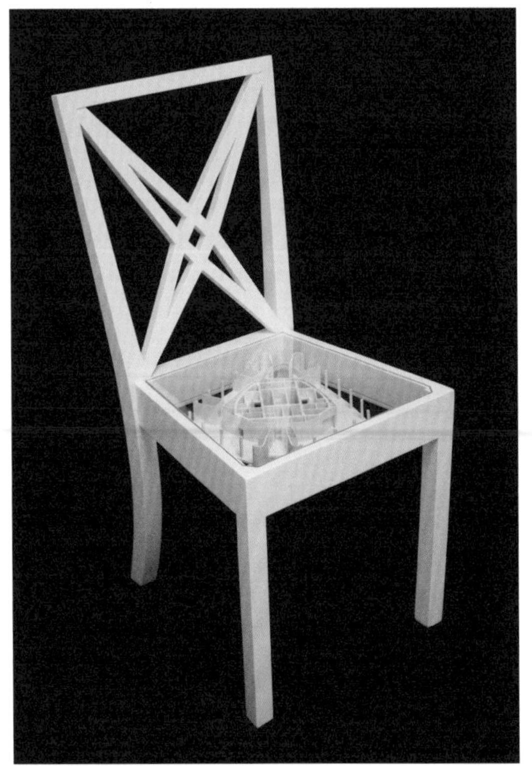

2

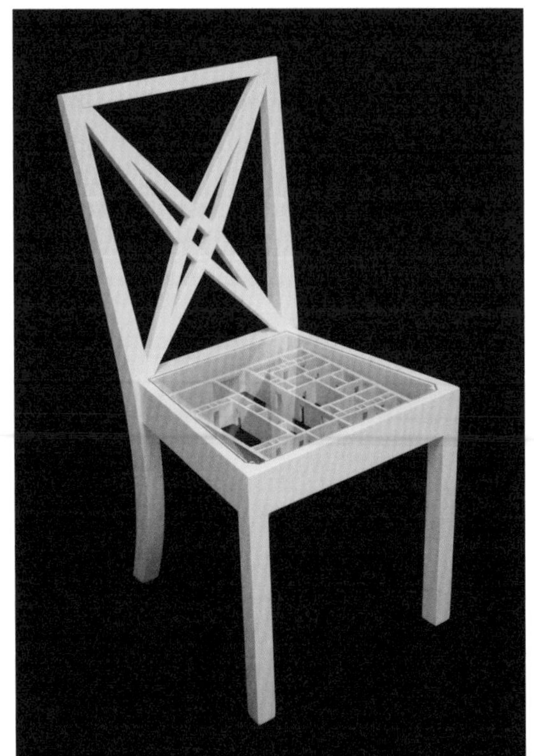

3

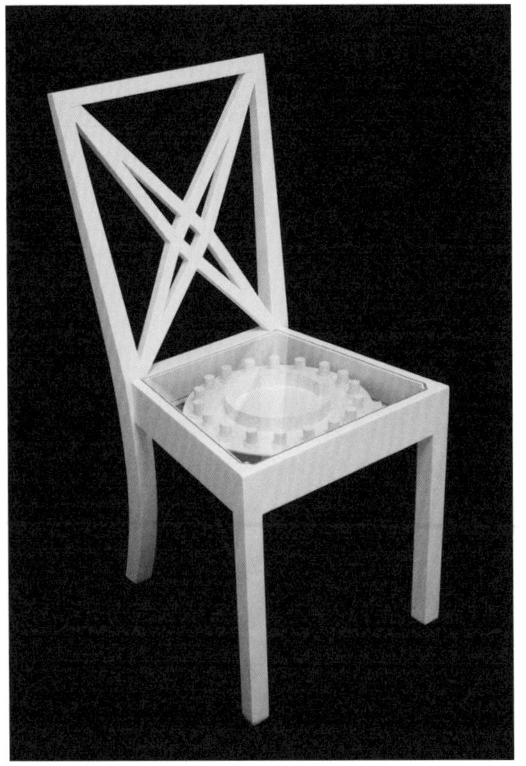

4

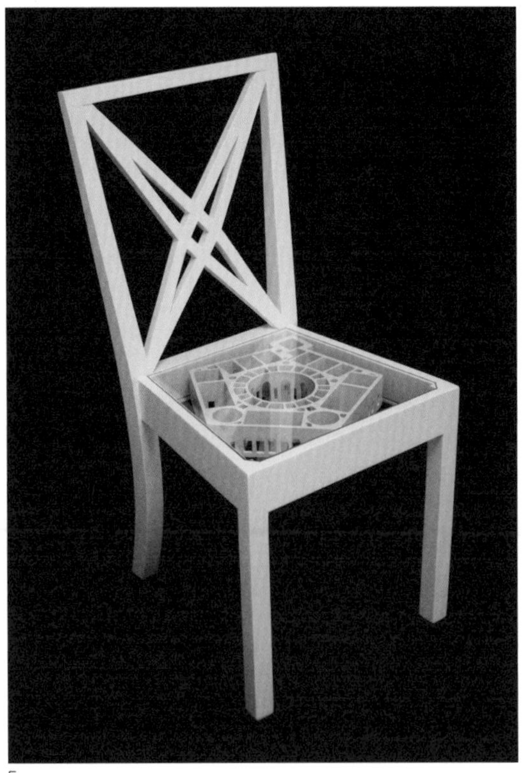

5

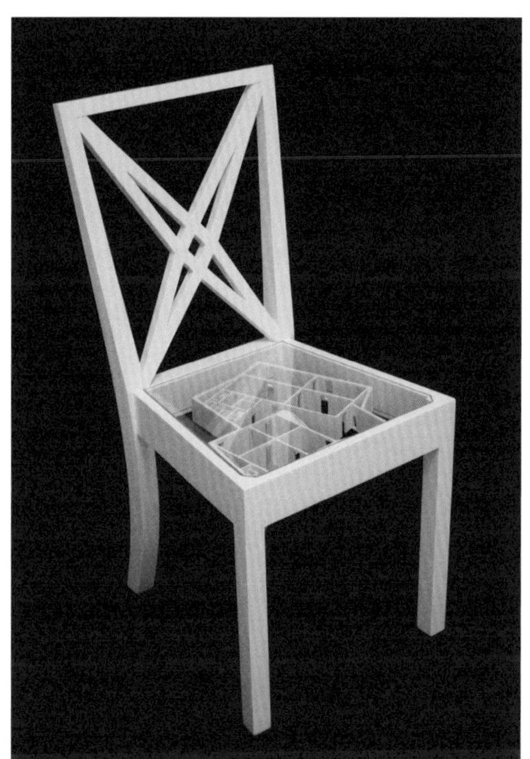
6

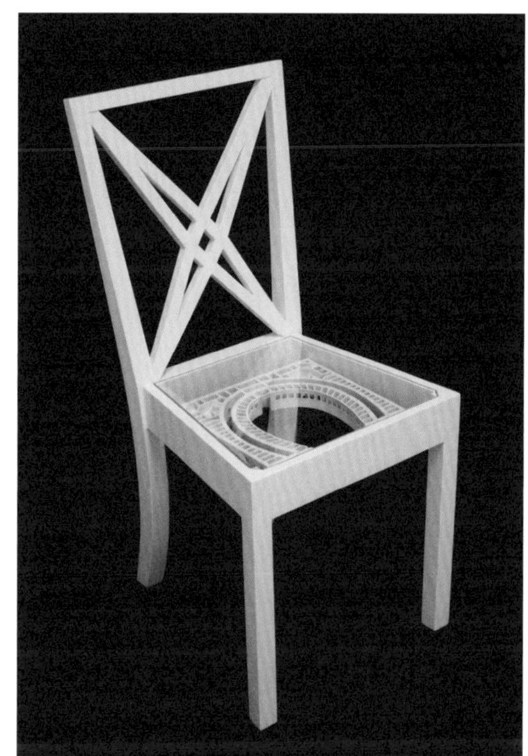
7

Grand Tour (details) 2020
2 Generali Tower, Milan
3 Kunsthaus, Zurich
4 Temple of Vesta, Tivoli
5 Villa Farnese, Caprarola
6 Kunstmuseum, Basel
7 La Scala, Milan

◇ You also made a series of *Burnt Interlocking Chairs* 1997. I wonder how you see the relationship between the two.

○ There's a kind balancing between the two series. It occurred to us subsequently that we made *Burnt Interlocking Chairs* during a moment of trauma in our professional life. We had made a couple of burnt chairs before this series, for example, *The Extent of the Fire* 1989 that showed the extent of the fire at the Houses of Parliament in 1834, and *Reichstag and Bundestag* 1989. But with the *Burnt Interlocking Chairs* there's a sense of us imagining or confronting our work as a ruin, that we are envisaging its destruction in some way. There's something obviously Soanean in that.

◇ There's the famous bird's-eye view of the Bank of England as a ruin drawn by J M Gandy, but Soane's obsession with the idea of the ruin ran far deeper. It was all about his legacy and his standing as an architect, and the fact he aspired to create buildings that rival those of imperial Rome. It was both self-effacing and grandiose. It's ironic that Soane's Bank of England did end up being demolished, only ninety years after his death.

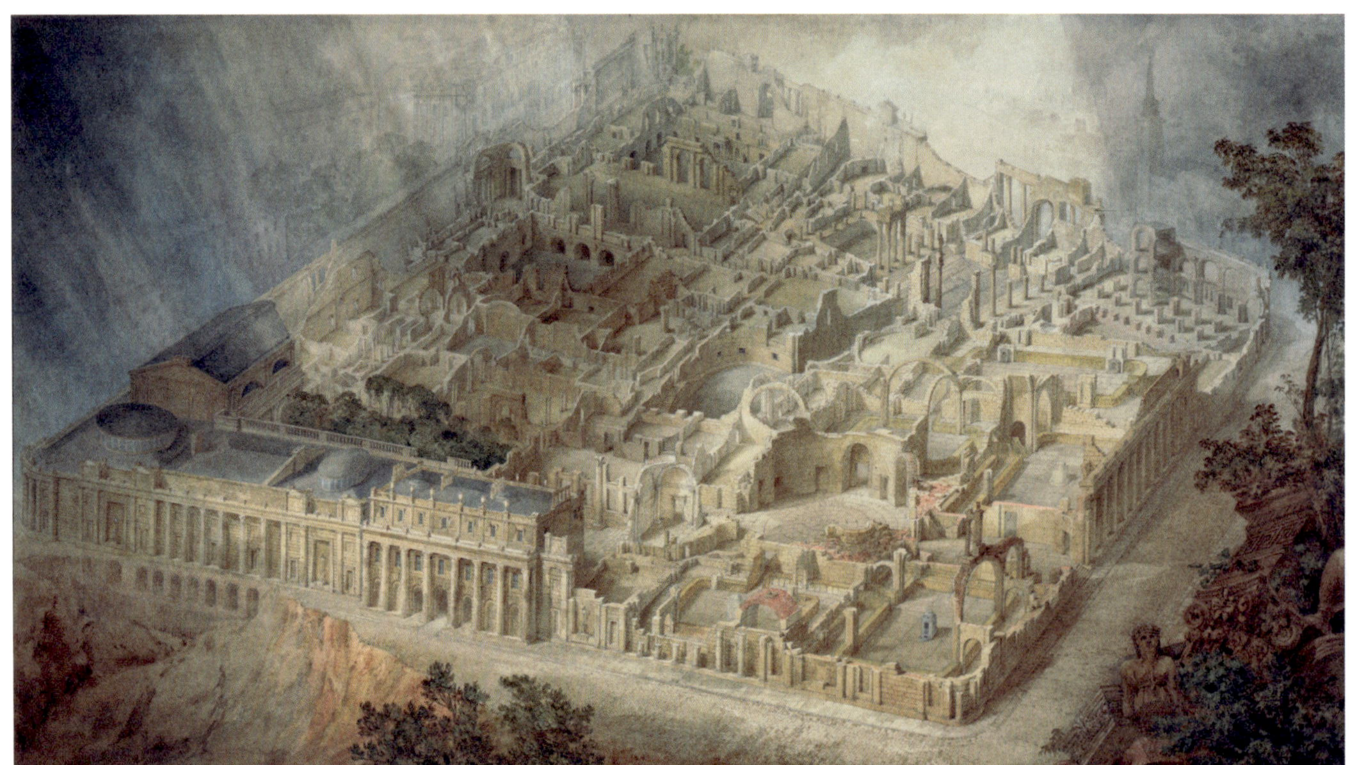

A Bird's-eye view of the Bank of England, Joseph Michael Gandy, 1830

Models for **Grand Tour** in the studio at Untitled, Kent, 2020

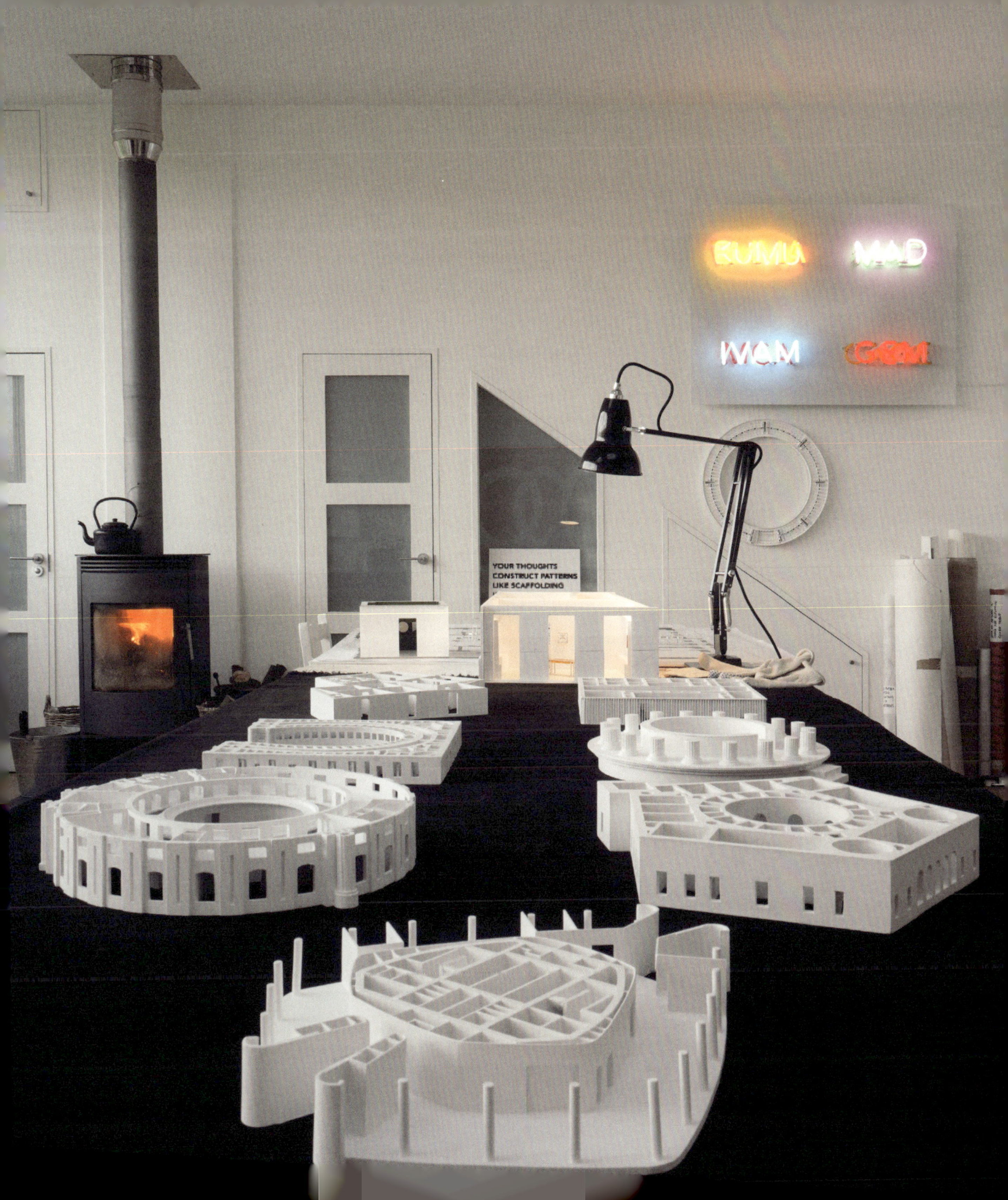
YOUR THOUGHTS
CONSTRUCT PATTERNS
LIKE SCAFFOLDING

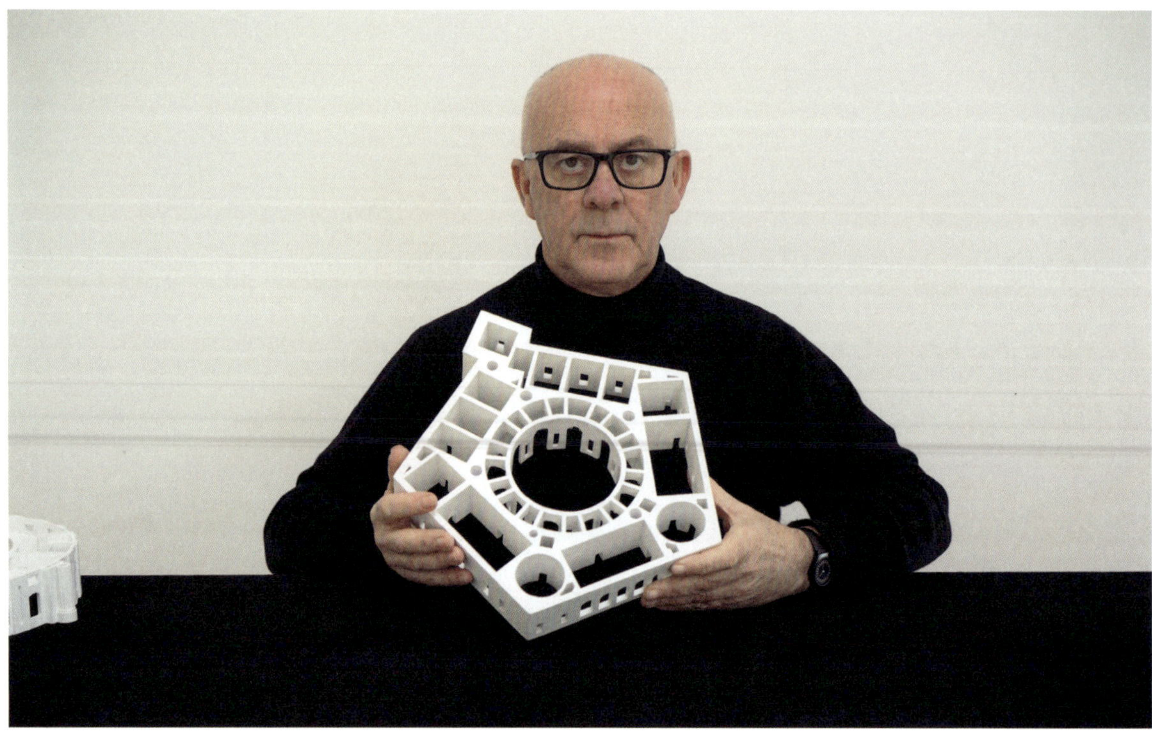

Ben Langlands with model of Villa Farnese, Caprarola, 2020

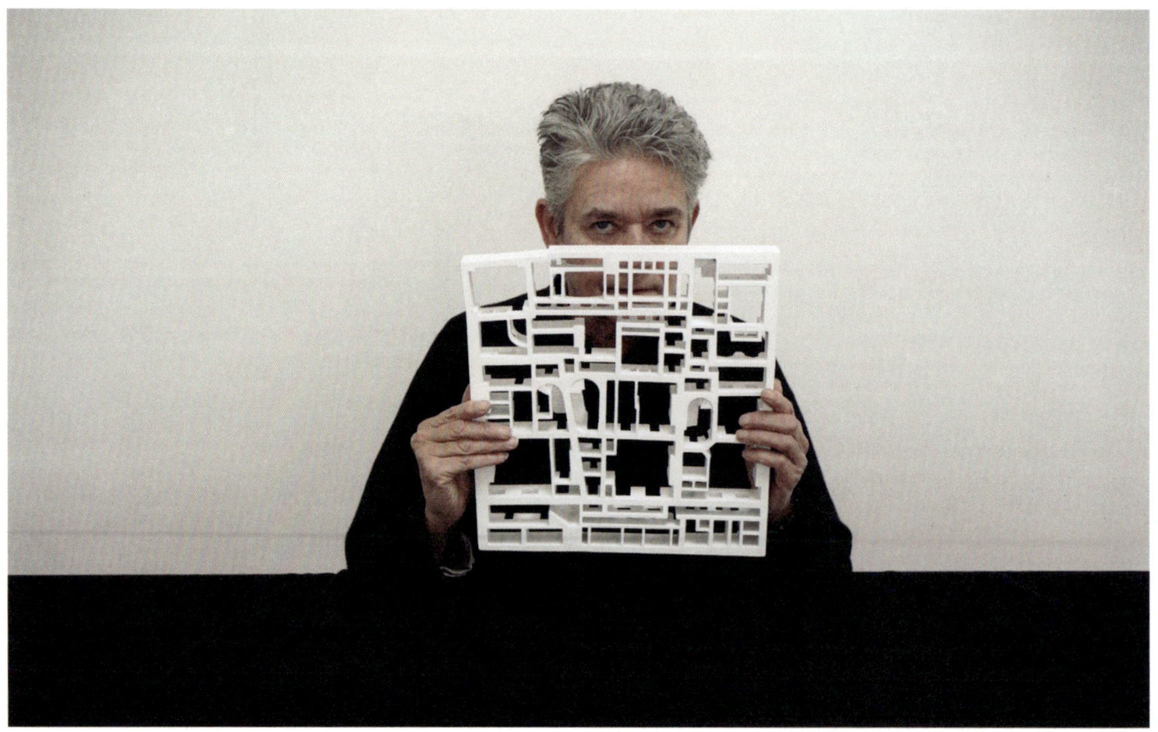

Nikki Bell with model of the basement of Sir John Soane's Museum, 2020

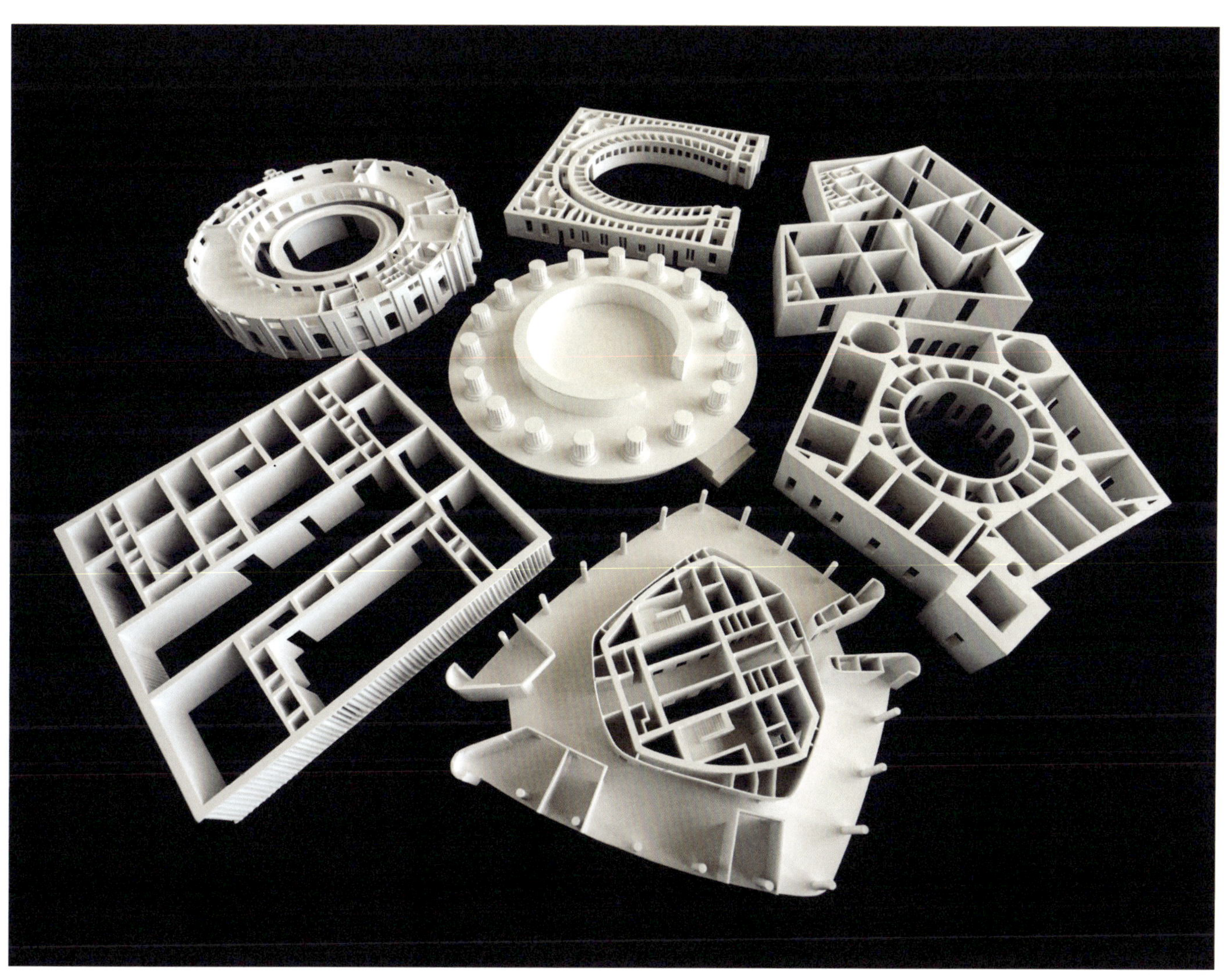

Detail of models for **Grand Tour** 2020
Clockwise from top: La Scala Theatre, Milan; Kunstmuseum, Basel; Villa Farnese, Caprarola; Generali Tower, Milan; Kunsthaus, Zurich; Bourse de Commerce: Collection Pinault, Paris. Centre: Temple of Vesta, Tivoli

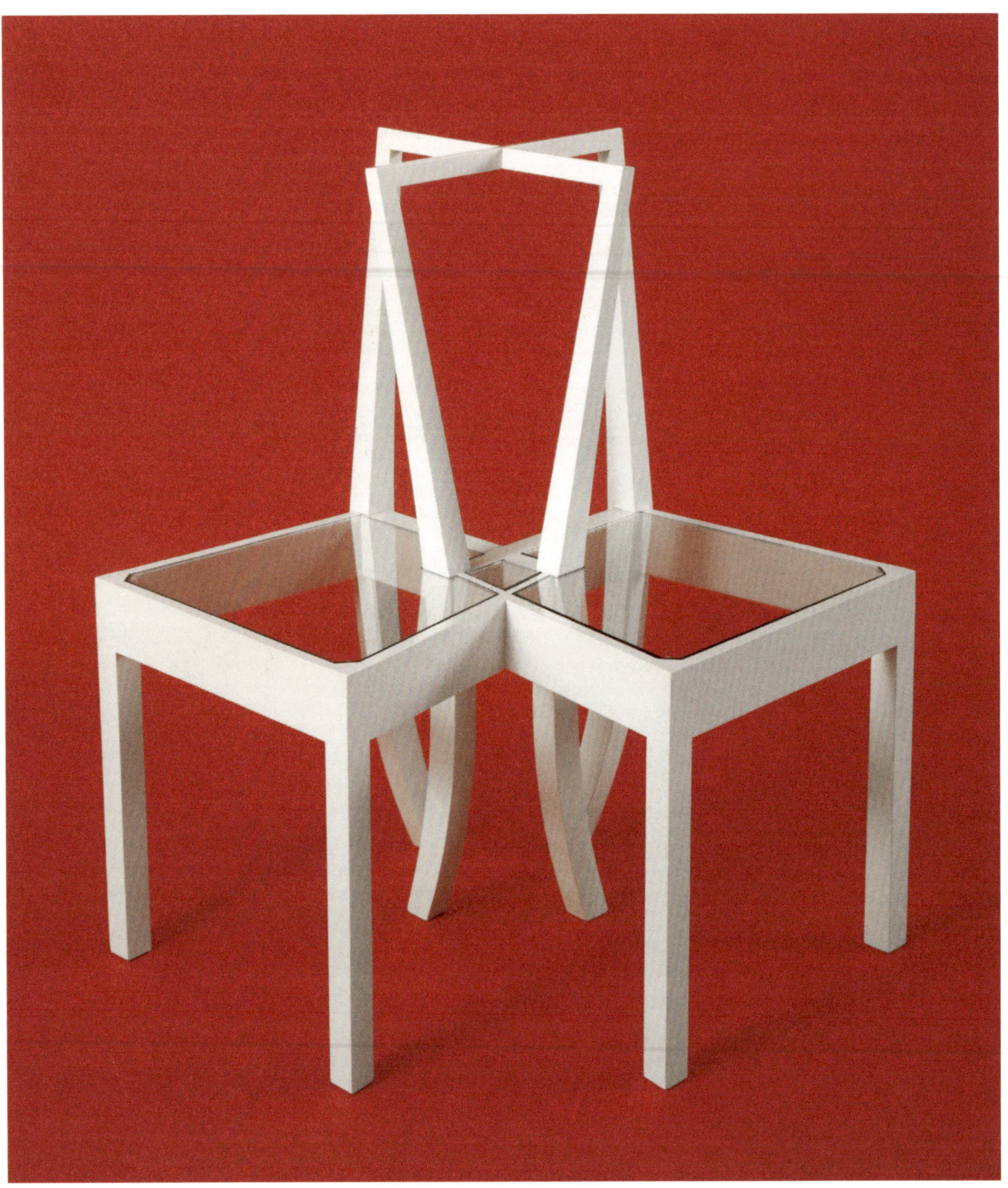

Interlocking Chairs 1995

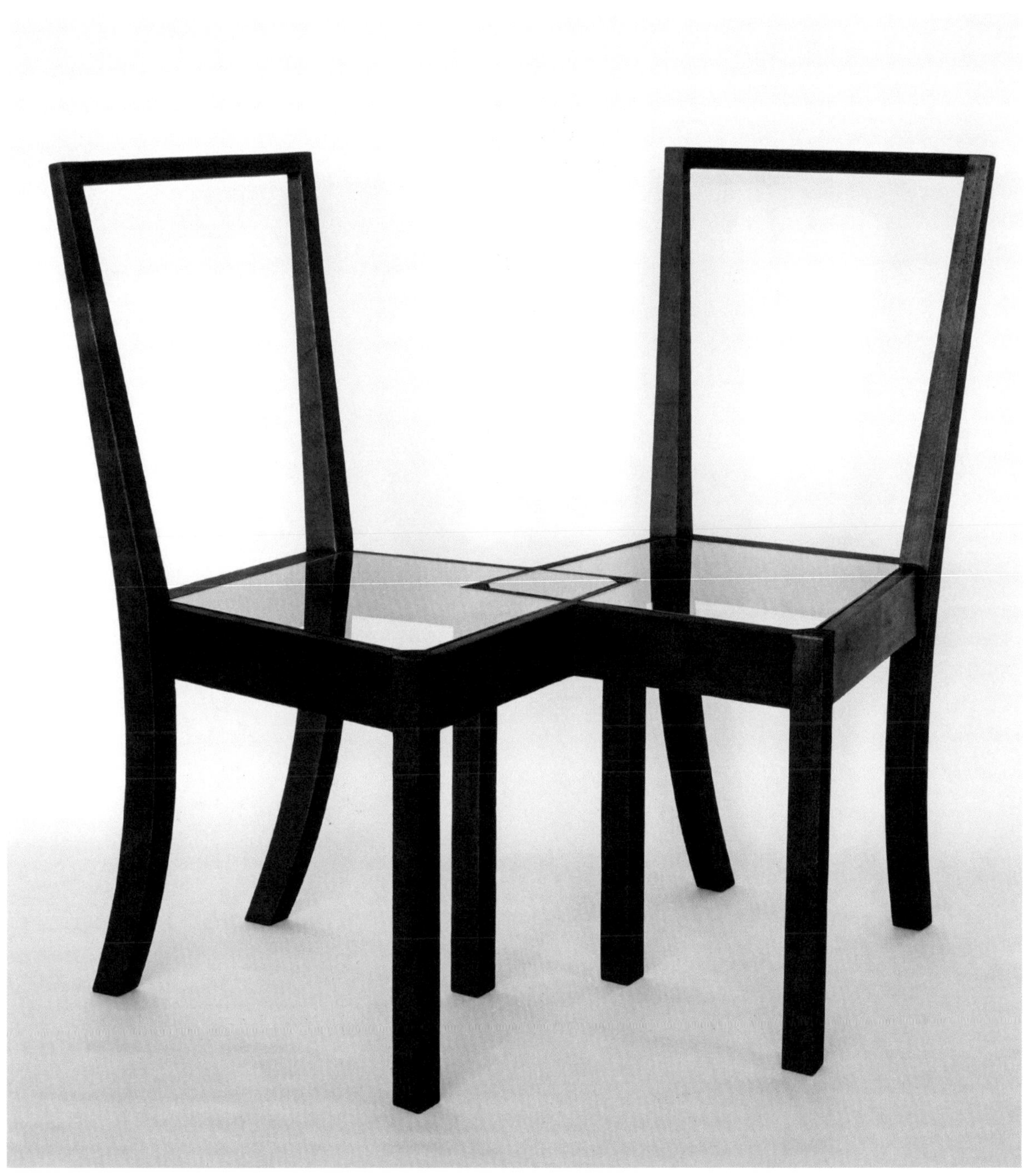

Burnt Interlocking Chairs 1997

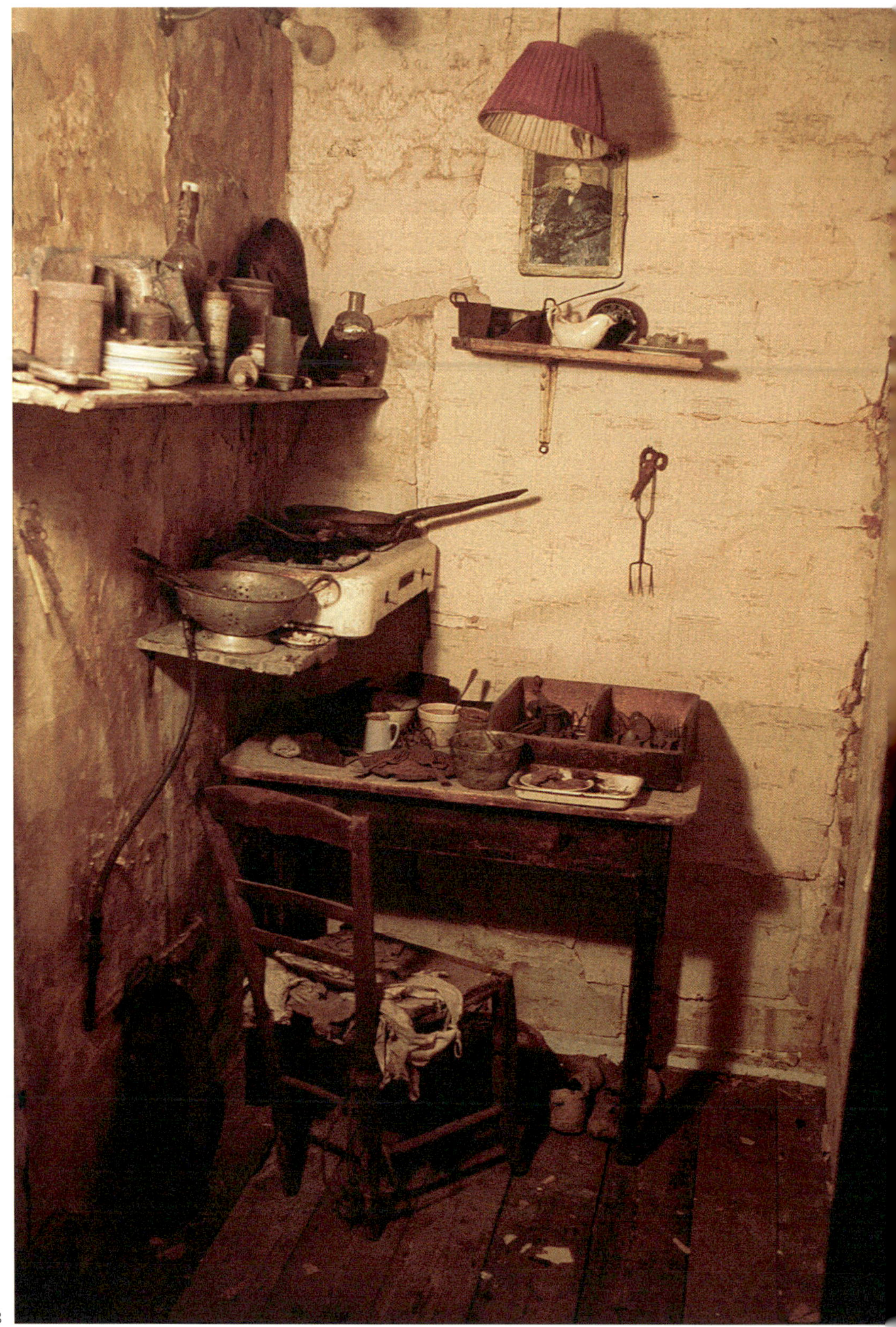

The Kitchen 1978

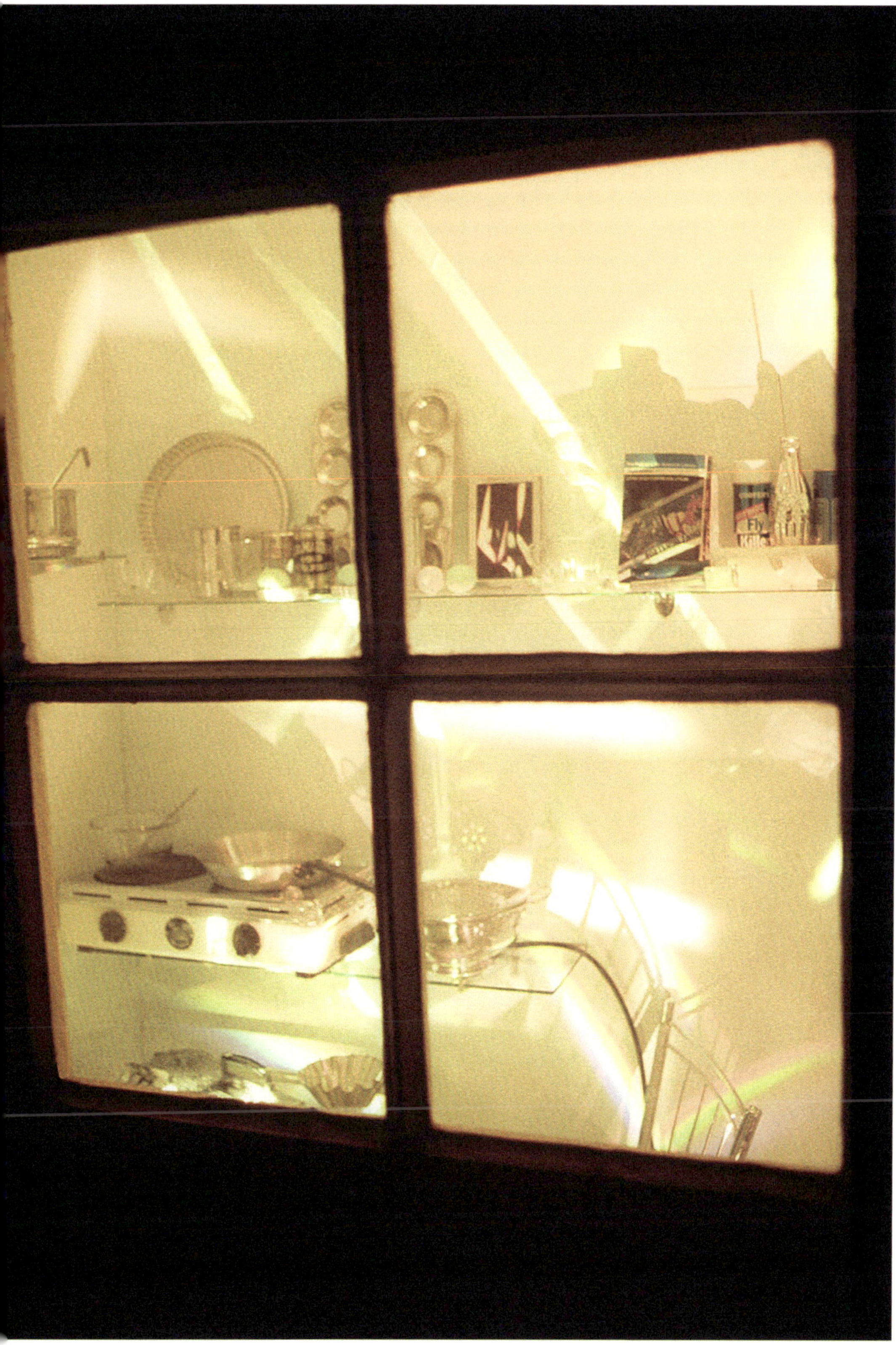
Fly

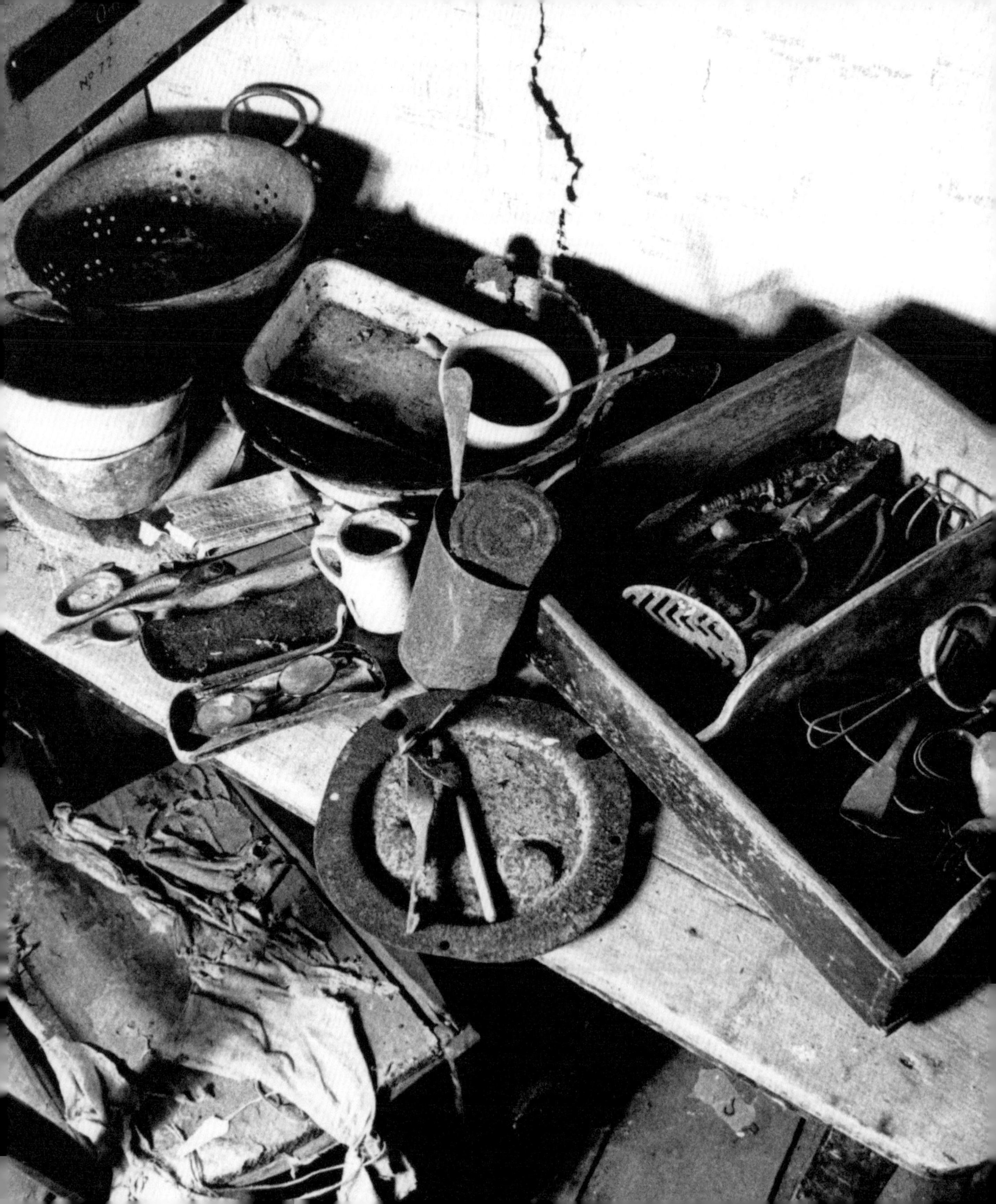
No 72

Collaboration

◇ I am interested in the collaborative nature of your practice, which is particularly fascinating in the context of a museum that is so obviously the product of one single person. How did your collaboration come about?

○ When we met and became friends, we discovered that although we had very different perspectives, we shared lots of interests and cared about things in the same way. We decided to test this out by making an artwork together. We made an installation called *The Kitchen* in 1978, which we then remade in 1980 for our degree show at Hornsey College of Art. It consisted of two kitchens that we built side-by-side – an old one and a new one. The idea was that Nikki would make the old one and Ben would make the new one.

We created the old kitchen using old objects that we found in ruins and abandoned houses in the East End: old cookers, broken down chairs and tables, old cutlery, broken crockery, bottles, pots and pans and what have you. We even carefully stripped wallpaper off damp walls and levered up old floorboards. We reinstalled all of this in a two-room structure that we built.

We conceived the new kitchen as a mirror image of the old kitchen in terms of the positioning of all the furniture and the objects within it. The idea was that you walked into the old kitchen where there were shelves laden with rotting and dirty old kitchen detritus. It smelled terrible. We even used the fat from the market café we used to frequent. It smelt of old beef dripping. And then you looked through the window into a brand-new kitchen with glass shelves, chrome furniture, a black-and-white vinyl tiled floor and lots of shiny objects. They were very cheap objects – often exactly the same objects that were in the old kitchen – but they were newly bought from pound shops and bargain stores. But you couldn't enter the new kitchen. You could only see it through the membrane of the window.

As we said, the original idea was that Nikki would make the old kitchen, and Ben would make the new kitchen. But in the end, we just found it easier to help each other, so we made the whole thing together, and then we photographed it and filmed it and carried on from there.

◇ So, there was a shift from a very structured collaboration to quite a fluid one.

○ In that work we were two people coming together intuitively and finding a way of working where we were in balance and could each bring different things to the collaboration. The outcomes were different than if we'd just been doing something on our own and richer in their associations, meanings and connections. We found that very exciting, and it's the same now. We're interested in

The Kitchen, detail of the old kitchen, 1978

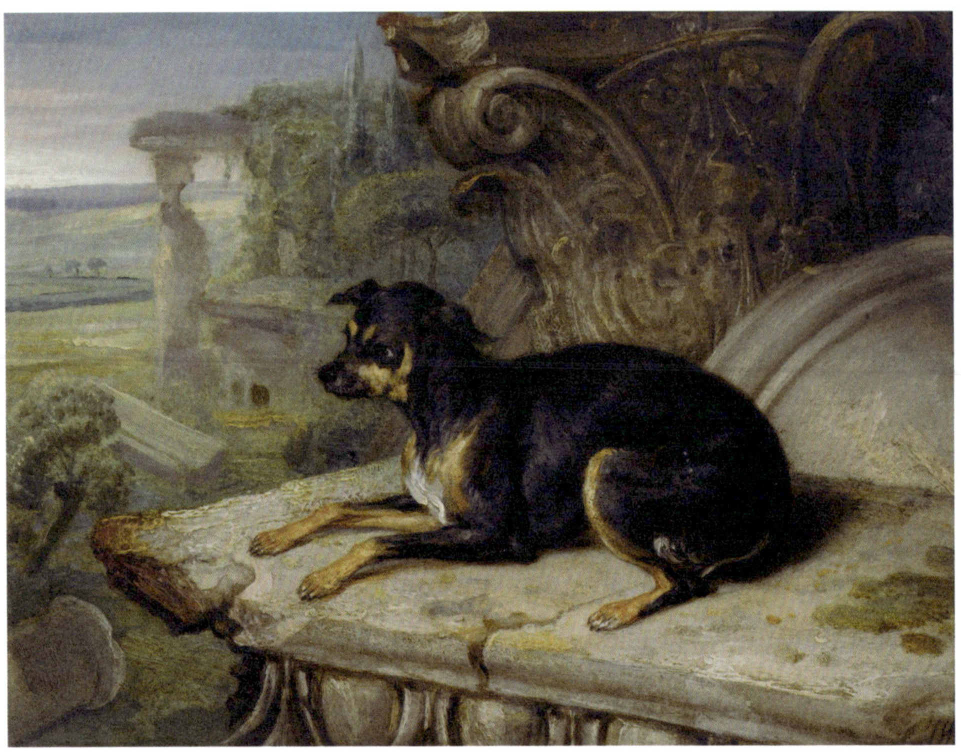

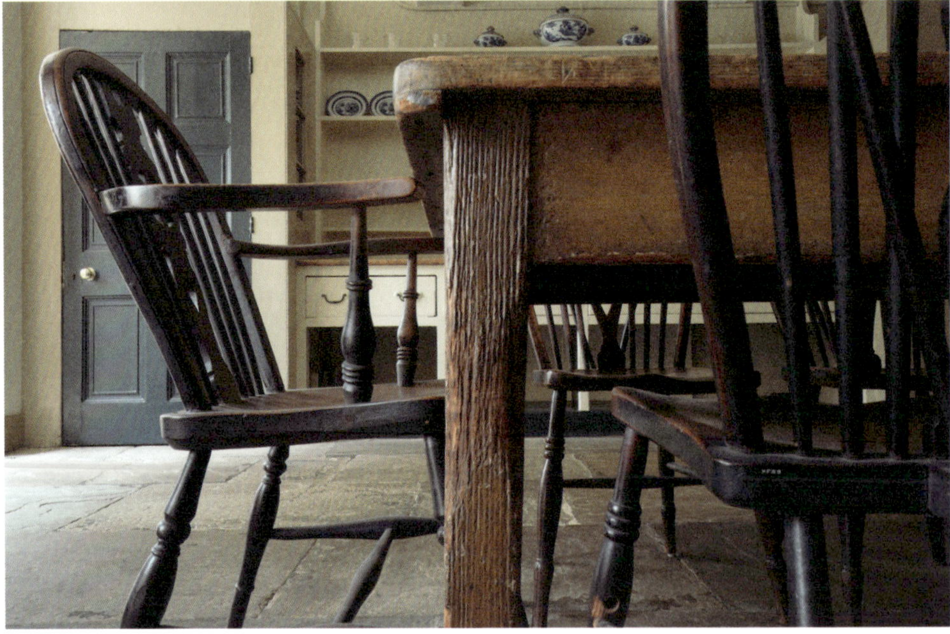

Painting of Fanny the dog by James Ward, 1822
Soane's kitchen table with table leg scratched by Fanny, Mrs Soane's Manchester terrier, 2019

things that we discover. We explore them and discuss them, and that leads to making art about them. It's quite a natural process.

◇ There are similarities here in how architects work together. There are some practices where the partners each have their own projects. They might discuss them with other partners and get their views, but fundamentally you know who is responsible for which building. Then there are far more fluid collaborations when what they produce is fundamentally different to what either one of them would create if they were working on their own. My favourite example of this is Castle Howard in Yorkshire – an early eighteenth-century Baroque palace designed by John Vanbrugh and Nicholas Hawksmoor. It doesn't look like Vanbrugh's later work and it doesn't look like Hawksmoor's either. It was that extraordinary and very rare thing: a meeting of minds over a few brief years before they started moving apart and heading in their own particular directions. To be able to sustain a collaboration of that nature for so long is unusual.

○ In the world of architecture there are, of course, lots of collaborations but lots of fallings out, as well. We always say, as long as it lasts; it's been 42 years so far. We're very different people, and we each bring very different things, but we have a common fascination with architecture and our relationships with people and our surroundings, which is at the core of everything we do. I think that's what's made what we do powerful.

With a lot of the tactics we use in our art – juxtaposing and combining, creating contrasts and revealing paradoxes – we find that having two people in the conversation multiplies what we can do in a way that's very natural. There's the nineteenth-century image of the artist in the garret struggling away on their own. But we don't really think that's relevant anymore. We find it much more interesting to collaborate; it's a perfectly normal way of working in other fields so why not in art.

◇ How do you think the dynamics of collaboration feed into the work you make?

○ We aim to make work that is resolved and homogenous, but which combines different elements, languages and media. We look for the medium that's right for the context in which we're working. We're always looking to be challenged: by ideas, propositions and settings, whether it's a project in Afghanistan, Japan, Rwanda, Ghana, or at the Soane Museum. We find it very interesting to work in places with such different histories and discover their impact on the present.

◇ Much of what you describe is also reflected in the range of scales that you turn your hands to: from the very small, right up to the scale of a building. With the latter, I am obviously referring to your house / studio *Untitled* in Kent. Is it a work of art or a work of architecture?

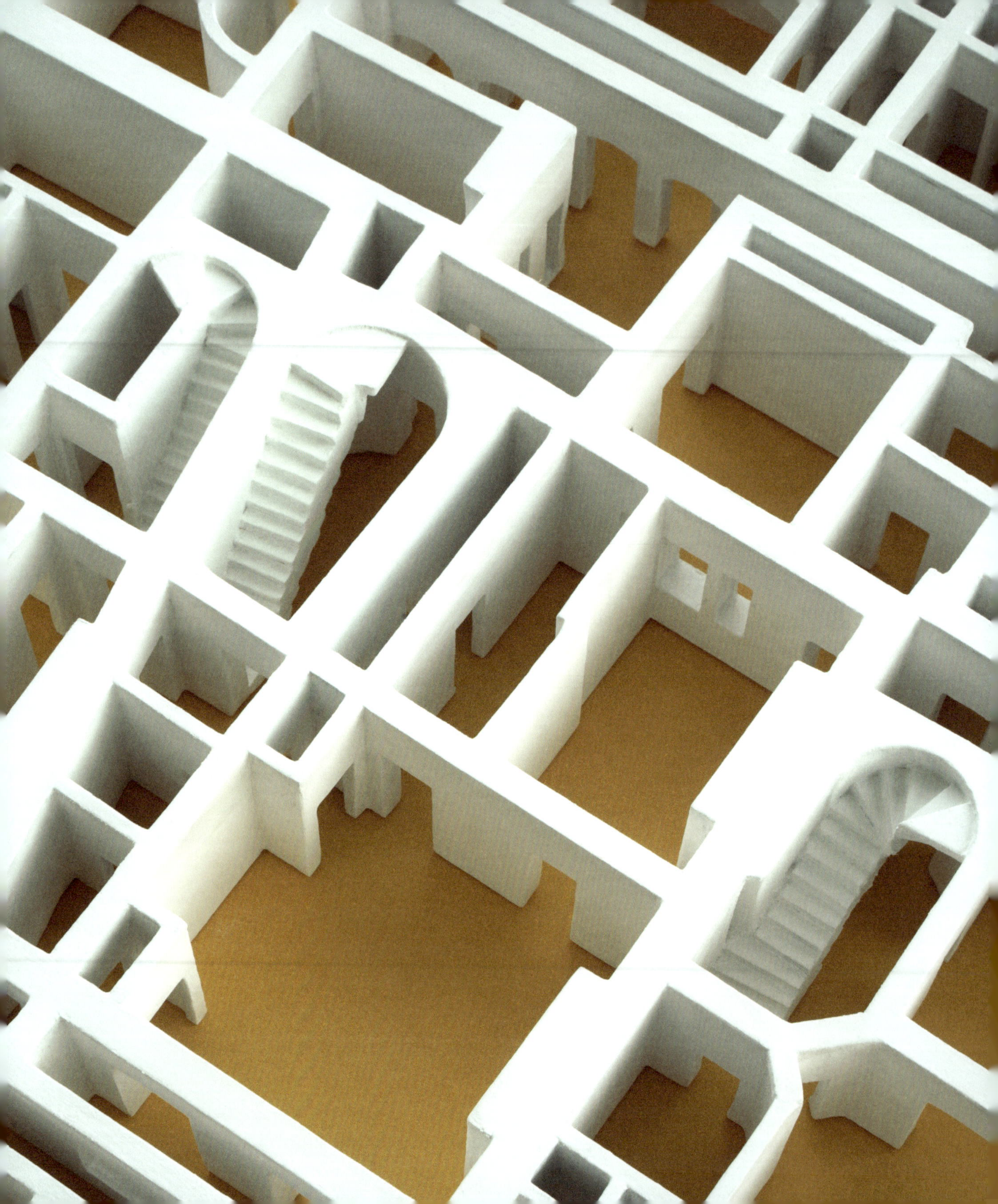

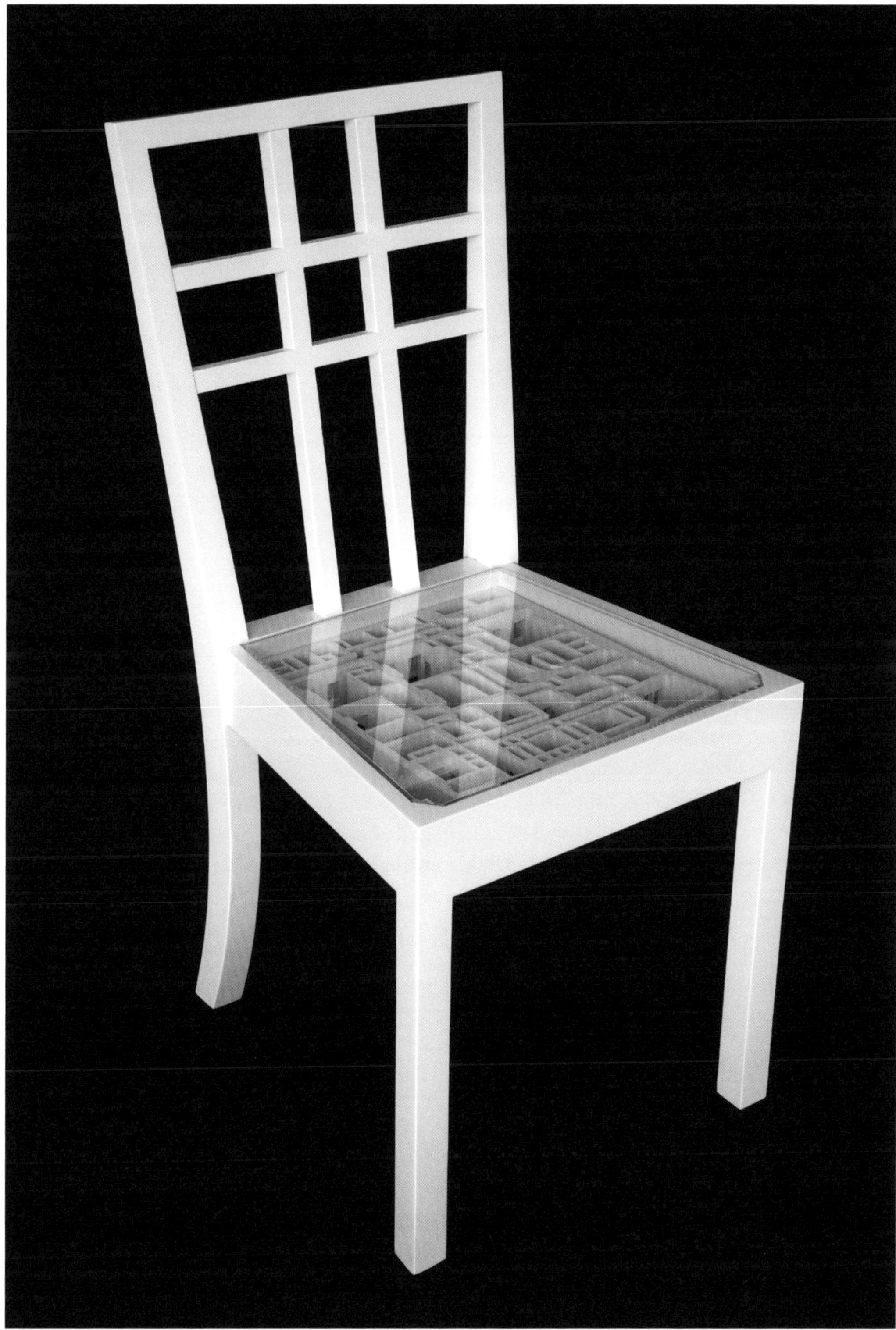

Traces of Living (detail) 2020
Left: Detail of model of the basement of Sir John Soane's Museum

○ That's a very good question. At a party we held there once, we remember the architect John Pawson turning to Deyan Sudjic, the former director of the Design Museum, and saying, 'this isn't architecture. This is an installation.' He's probably right. We wouldn't say it's architecture, because we're not architects and we don't think like architects. But it also depends on how you define architecture. It's a building and it's used for living and working in and we worked with engineers Atelier One to make sure it won't fall down.

◇ How did the project come about?

○ It was a very spontaneous decision to build it. We weren't planning on building somewhere outside London, and we weren't looking for anywhere when we stumbled on the piece of land that we eventually bought. We'd rebuilt and restored our house and studio in Whitechapel, but we hadn't built anything completely from scratch before. It was exciting to demolish the existing shack on the site and start from nothing. It was also tough, because while we built the house, we didn't have electricity and we had to learn how to live without the usual utilities and infrastructures that we normally rely on. We loved the location and created a house that is deliberately very discreet, we wanted it to disappear in a way.

Where we live and work has always been a continuum. We've always very carefully considered the houses and studios we've lived and worked in and modified and adjusted them to make them reflect what we want. This is about incorporating our emotional and imaginative life into them as well as our practical, day-to-day needs and requirements. *Untitled* is no different in that respect. It's a kind of continuous artwork in the form of a building.

◇ And very like the Soane Museum in that regard. One of the ways of conceiving the Museum is not as a building in a conventional sense, but as a model that just happens to exist at full-scale. Is that a useful way of understanding *Untitled* too?

○ Yes, there's something in that. It's also about the simplicity of the materials we've used. It's a very pared-down palette: just oak – there's a lot of oaks surrounding us – glass and aluminium. The palette was very much an artistic choice, as opposed to an architectural one. It was conceived to be very sensitive to where we were located; we didn't want to start chopping down any trees surrounding us.

It's also reflected in terms of how the building is used; it's not very domestic. It doesn't really have any domestic furniture in it. It has a dining table and chairs, which we designed ourselves, and various work surfaces, but there are no sofas or televisions or things like that.

So, maybe, it's a little like Pitzhanger Manor, the country house Soane built in Ealing, when it was still on the edge of London. It's a villa, a retreat rather than a home, somewhere for entertaining, usually for leisure, though sometimes also for work, a place where life plays out at a different pace.

Untitled is also a place where we display our work – old and new – and where we invite people to come and see what we're doing. We like it to reflect who we are. At the moment, in the lead-up to this exhibition at the Soane, and another we're working on in Ghana, the building is completely turned over to making work. It's just a studio with a kitchen and a bedroom attached to it. But when the exhibitions are over, it can turn into something else. We'll use it just for displaying work and we'll invite some people over and relax until the next exhibition comes along.

1
Was Modelle Konnen – Eine Kleine Geshichte Architekturmodells in der Zeitgenossischen Kunst (What Models Can Do – A Short History of the Architectural Model in Contemporary Art) MGK Museum für Gegenwartskunst Siegen, Germany

Following pages
Untitled, Kent, 2019

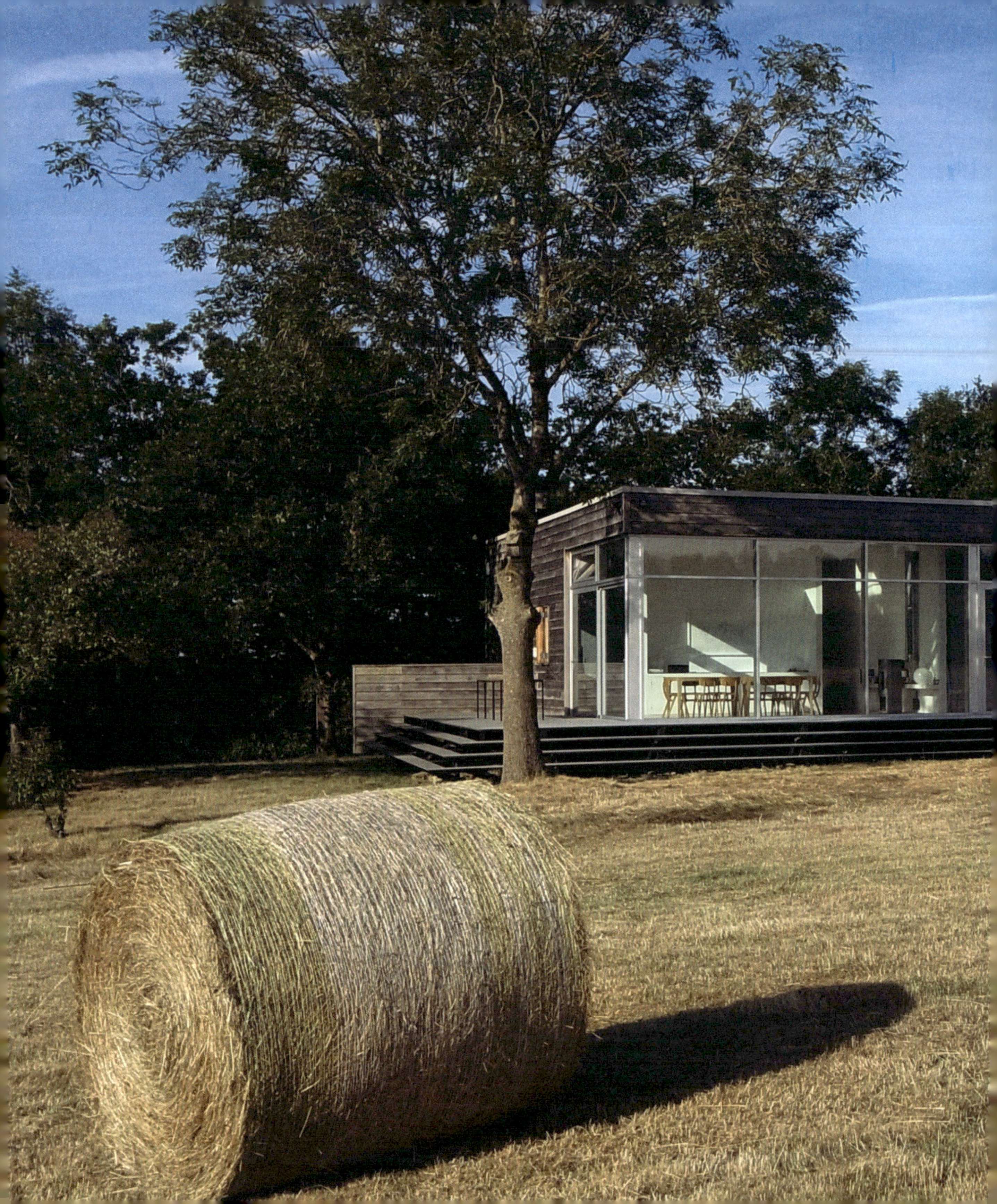

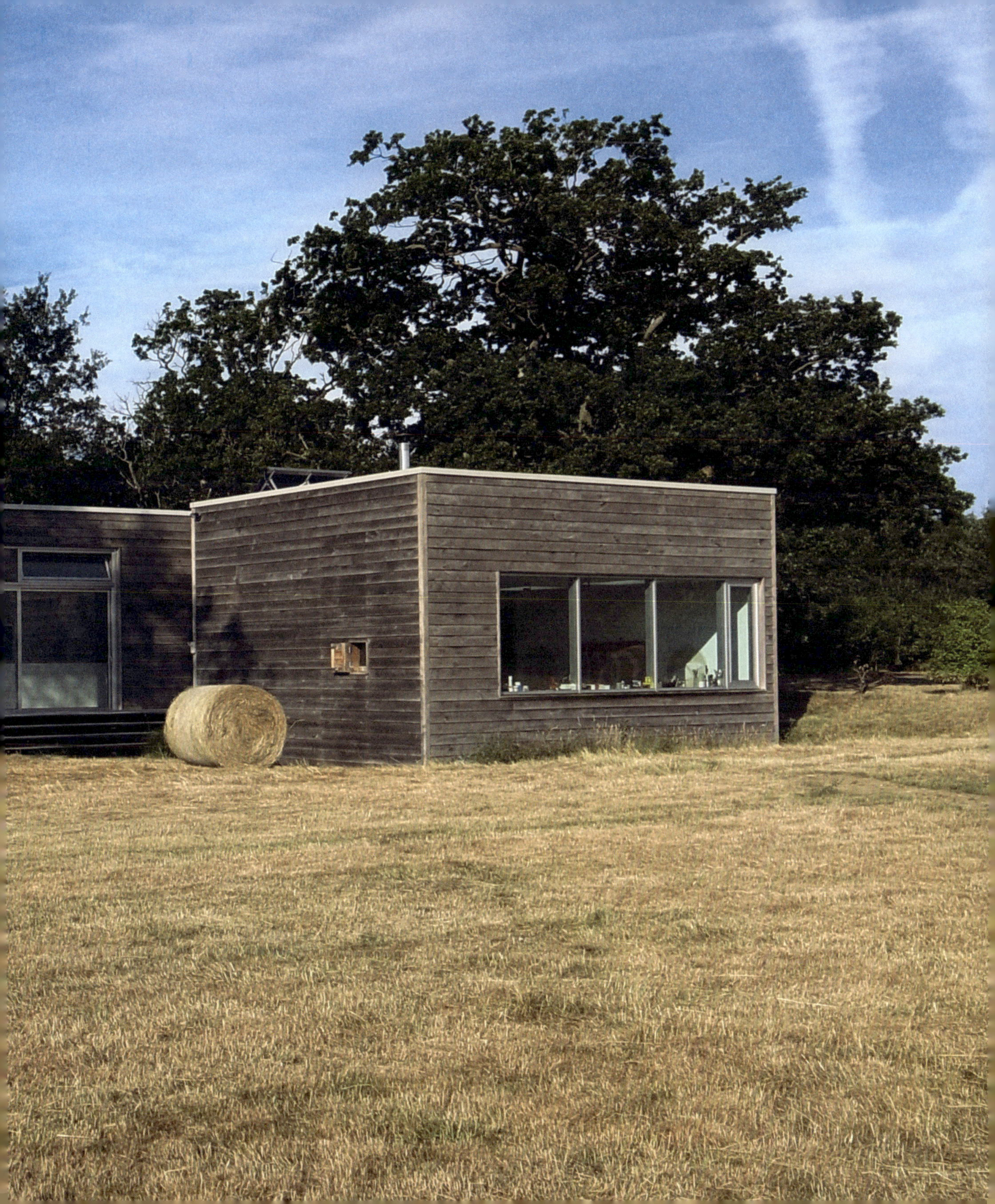

List of Works

Front Kitchen
Traces of Living 1986–2020
Beech, MDF, found objects, glass, AC lacquer
Installation: chairs: 92 × 45 × 45 cm (each); table: 90 × 137 × 74 cm
The artists
pp.14–15, 40, 89

Wind Dried Whippet 1982
Desiccated dog carcass
67 × 107 × 15 cm
The artists
p.47

Back Kitchen
The House of Osama bin Laden 2003
Interactive computer animation/data projection
The artists
p.35

Crypt
Burnt Interlocking Chairs 1997
Charred beech, glass
92 × 92 × 64 cm
The artists
p.81

Monk's Parlour
Burnt Madonna 1985
Charred oak
125 × 40 × 35 cm
The artists
p.49

The Foyle Space
Museums in Motion 1989
Wood, paint, glass, lacquer
77 × 322 × 13 cm overall
DJ Lockhart, London
p.18

Infinite Loop 2014
Wood, aluminium, acrylic sheet, paint, lacquer
3 panels: 80 × 80 × 9 cm each; 80 × 240 × 9 cm overall
The artists
pp.19–21

Millbank Penitentiary 1994
Wood, glass, aluminium, paint, lacquer
112 × 112 × 16 cm
Ipswich City Museum & Art Gallery, Ipswich
p.16

13 Breakfast Room
Globe Table 2020
Wood, lacquer, resin
120 (h) × 110 (dia) cm
The artists
p.52

Virtual World, Medal of Dishonour 2008
Struck and enamelled silver
Diameter 7.5 cm
The artists
pp.63, 64–65

Library-Dining Room
Grand Tour 2020
Wood, lacquer, glass
Installation: 92 × 800 × 45cm; chairs: 92 × 45 × 45 cm (each)
The artists
pp.71 detail Bourse de Commerce Collection Pineault, 72–75

***www.** 2000
Laser etched optical glass
10 × 10 × 10 cm
The artists

South Drawing Room
Conversation Seat 1986*
Wood, glass, lacquer
70 × 110 × 50 cm
The artists
*Artists' copy of the original which is in the collection of the Norwegian National Museum of Contemporary Art, Oslo
p.50

North Drawing Room
Interlocking Chairs 1995
Wood, lacquer, glass
60 × 60 × 45 cm
Private collection, London
p.80

South Exhibition Gallery
Adjoining Rooms 1989
Wood, glass, acrylic sheet, AC lacquer
Installation: 78 × 426 × 62 cm; three items: 78 × 142 × 62 cm (each)
Tate, London
p.51

Marseille, Cité Radieuse 2001
Wood, aluminium, glass, lacquer
102 × 200 × 10 cm
Southampton City Art Gallery, Southampton
p.27

Council of Europe 1989
Wood, glass, paint, AC lacquer
60 × 60 × 15 cm
The artists
p.62

***Apple, Sunny Vale** 2018
MDF, paper, card, paint, acrylic
91 × 91 × 7.5 cm
The artists

***Apple, Cupertino** 2018
MDF, paper, card, paint, acrylic
91 × 91 × 7.5 cm
The artists

Logo Works 1998–99
4 screen prints on Somerset Satin 300 gsm paper
70 × 70 cm each
Cristea Roberts Gallery, London
p.29

Apple Oblique (green) 2015
Archival pigment print on Hahnemuhle Photo Rag 310 gsm
75 × 75 cm
Cristea Roberts Gallery, London
p.23

Nvidia, Santa Clara (orange) 2015
Archival pigment print on Hahnemuhle Photo Rag 310 gsm
75 × 75 cm
Cristea Roberts Gallery, London
p.24

North Exhibition Gallery

Model for Adjoining Rooms 1989
Wood, MDF, card, poly carbonate, paint, acrylic sheet
15 × 54 × 15 cm (dimensions include acrylic case)
Derwent London plc
p.30

***Model for Interlocking Chairs** 1994
MDF, card, paint, acrylic sheet
15 × 60 × 15 cm (dimensions include acrylic case)
Derwent London plc

***Model for Burnt Interlocking Chairs** 1997
MDF, card, paint, acrylic sheet
15 × 60 × 15 cm (dimensions include acrylic case)
Derwent London plc

Façade Berlin 1999
Wood, glass, paint, lacquer
112 × 98 × 13 cm
Christina and Dimitri Goulandris Collection, London
p.28

Frozen Sky (Night & Day) 2000
2 screen process prints on Somerset satin 300 gsm
70 × 66 cm each
Cristea Roberts Gallery, London
pp.59 (Day) and 60 (Night)

Air Routes of Europe (Night & Day) 2002–20
Archival pigment print
100 × 100 cm
The artists
pp.56 (Night) and 57 (Day)

Air Routes of Britain (Night & Day) 2000
2 screen prints on Somerset satin 300 gsm
70 × 55 cm each
The artists
pp.54 (Night) and 55 (Day)

* works in the show but not illustrated in this publication

Following page
Untitled, Kent, 2019

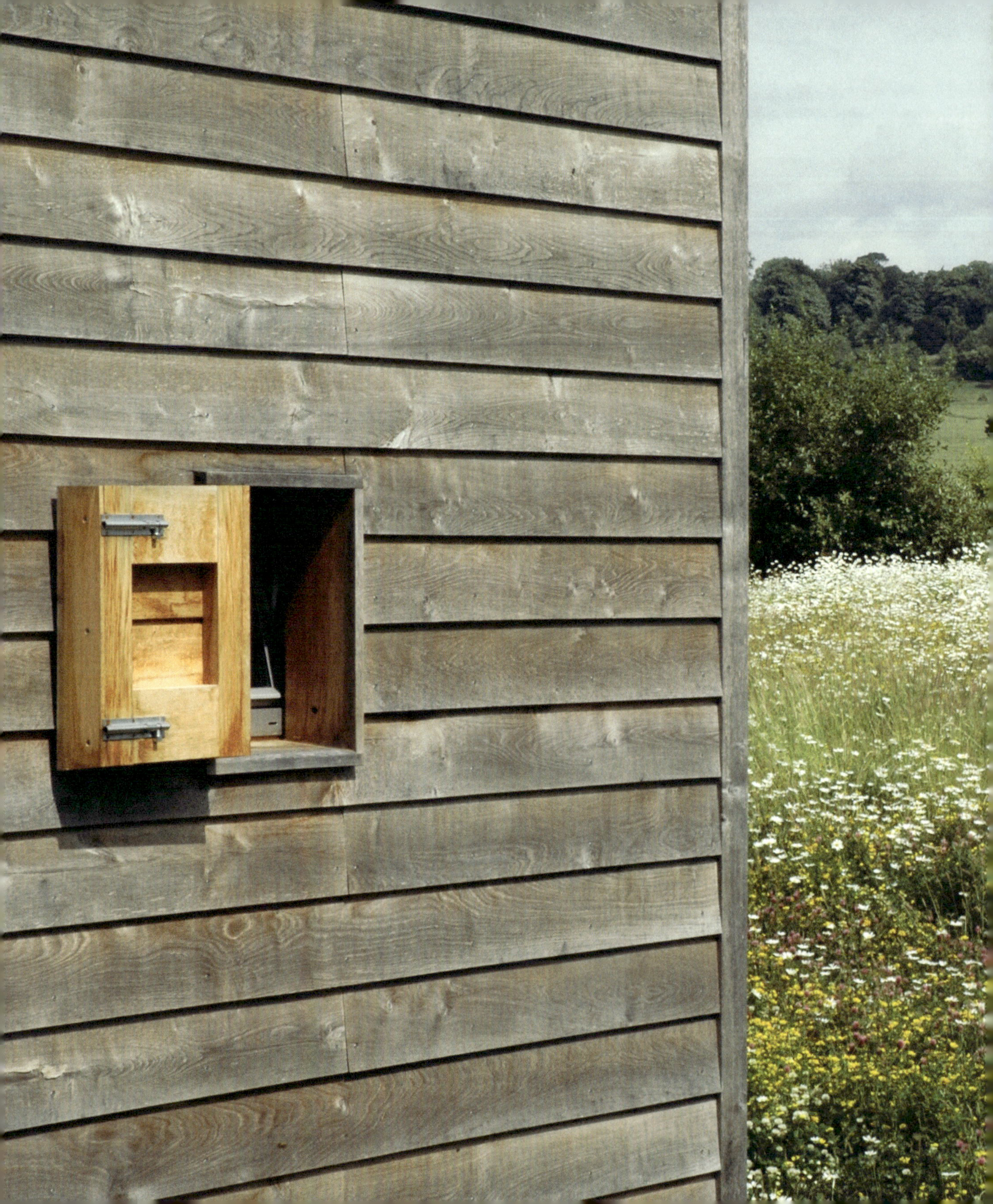